Hypnotherapy
Children's W

Hypnotherapy Scripts to Promote Children's Wellbeing is a collection of tried-and-tested scripts that will aid hypnotherapists in developing and implementing treatment plans for promoting the wellbeing of children.

The book offers a variety of approaches solely focussed on children (aged 5 to 17 years), including: Ericksonian approaches utilising metaphors and story-telling; solution-focussed approaches; benefits approaches; parts therapy; Gestalt therapy and regression therapy. The scripts are intended to help deal with issues relevant to children such as lack of confidence; low self-esteem or self-worth; negative image; lack of motivation; anxiety (general, social and exam); learning and recalling information; fears; phobias; habits; sleep issues; bullying; abuse; bereavement and loss.

Serving as a unique resource of techniques and compiled from the author's years of personal experience, this book is beneficial for students, newly qualified and experienced hypnotherapists alike.

Jacki Pritchard works as a clinical hypnotherapist, independent social worker and trainer in social care. She offers hypnotherapy services to children and adults in two practice locations, schools and colleges through her company Jacki Pritchard Ltd.

Hypnotherapy Scripts to Promote Children's Wellbeing

Jacki Pritchard

LONDON AND NEW YORK

First published 2021
by Routledge
2 Park Square, Milton Park, Abingdon, Oxon OX14 4RN

and by Routledge
52 Vanderbilt Avenue, New York, NY 10017

Routledge is an imprint of the Taylor & Francis Group, an informa business

© 2021 Jacki Pritchard

The right of Jacki Pritchard to be identified as author of this work has been asserted by her in accordance with sections 77 and 78 of the Copyright, Designs and Patents Act 1988.

All rights reserved. No part of this book may be reprinted or reproduced or utilised in any form or by any electronic, mechanical, or other means, now known or hereafter invented, including photocopying and recording, or in any information storage or retrieval system, without permission in writing from the publishers.

Trademark notice: Product or corporate names may be trademarks or registered trademarks, and are used only for identification and explanation without intent to infringe.

British Library Cataloguing-in-Publication Data
A catalogue record for this book is available from the British Library

Library of Congress Cataloging-in-Publication Data
Names: Pritchard, Jacki, author.
Title: Hypnotherapy scripts to promote children's wellbeing / Jacki Pritchard.
Description: Abingdon, Oxon; New York, NY: Routledge, 2020. | Includes index. | Identifiers: LCCN 2020014259 (print) | LCCN 2020014260 (ebook) | ISBN 9780367490393 (hardback) | ISBN 9780367490386 (paperback) | ISBN 9781003044147 (ebook)
Subjects: LCSH: Hypnotism–Therapeutic use. | Child psychotherapy.
Classification: LCC RJ505.H86 P75 2020 (print) | LCC RJ505.H86 (ebook) | DDC 615.8/512083–dc23
LC record available at https://lccn.loc.gov/2020014259
LC ebook record available at https://lccn.loc.gov/2020014260

ISBN: 9780367490393 (hbk)
ISBN: 9780367490386 (pbk)
ISBN: 9781003044147 (ebk)

Typeset in Sabon
by Deanta Global Publishing Services, Chennai, India

Printed in the United Kingdom
by Henry Ling Limited

This book is dedicated to my granddaughter
Grace Ava
May your imagination always take you to wonderful places

Contents

1	Introduction: Hypnotherapy, children and wellbeing	1
2	How to use the scripts *Appendix 1: Summary of what the scripts cover 12*	6
3	Just imagine *Script 1: Fancy dress show 21* *Script 2: The sandpit 22* *Script 3: Bubbles 23*	21
4	Travelling glow: Colour relaxation	24
5	Exploring the island in the city	27
6	The flea market	30
7	Relaxing on the riverbank: Having some quiet time	32
8	Fire *Script 1: Fire in the living room 35* *Script 2: Camp fire 36* *Additional script 1: Burning stuff 37* *Additional script 2: Fireworks and the rocket 37*	35
9	The maze *Additional script 1: Deepening in the maze 41*	39
10	The beards	42
11	Traffic lights	44
12	The workshop	46

13 A bit of stomping   49

14 The clock   52

15 Going back in time   55
    Script 1: The castle and drawbridge 55
    Script 2: The train 56

16 Star in the sky   58
    Additional script 1: Exploring the moon 59
    Additional script 2: Swinging to sleep 59
    Additional script 3: Looking for the spiritual star 60

17 Harry the heron   61

18 Bertie the beagle   63

19 Chinga the cat   66

20 The salmon triplets   69

21 Maurice the mole   71

22 Harriet the hedgehog   75

23 Bees in the hives   79

24 Butterflies passing by   82
    Additional script 1: Remembering and commemorating 84
    Additional Script 2: Rex the rat's letter to his mum and dad 85

25 Lily Lavender's Wellbeing Shop   86
    Additional script 1: The relaxing candle wax 88
    Additional script 2: Wash it away 88
    Additional script 3: Bottle of confidence (or motivation, determination
        or something else relevant for the child) *89*
    Additional script 4: Lily Lavender's wellbeing assessment 89
    Appendix 1: How to do the assessment of wellbeing 90
    Appendix 2: Assessment of wellbeing form 91

26 The Fairy House   93

27 Getting rid of stuff at the business centre   96

28	The post office	98
	Additional script 1: Draw or paint a picture 99	
	Additional script 2: Writing a letter 100	
	Additional script 3: Posting a parcel 100	
	Additional script 4: Invisible bubble wrap 101	
29	The art gallery	103
	Additional script 1: Self-portrait 105	
	Additional script 2: An exhibition – The life of … 105	
	Additional script 3: Painting the walls 107	
30	The bakery	108
	Additional script 1: Baking a banana cake 110	
31	The climbing wall	112
32	Bennett's Bicycle Shop	115
	Additional script 1: Going for a ride 117	
33	Storing and recalling	118
	Script 1: The library 118	
	Script 2: The archives 121	
	Additional Script 1: Books and messages 122	
34	The spa	124
35	The igloo	128
36	Spencer the singer-songwriter	130
	Index	133

Chapter 1

Introduction
Hypnotherapy, children and wellbeing

Main objective in writing this book

This book focuses on presenting scripts which can be used when working with children to promote their wellbeing. My main aim in putting this collection together in a book was to provide a resource of ready-made scripts, which have been regularly tried and tested. I also wanted the book to be different in its format in that it would not be an academic text going through the usual subject areas one finds in hypnotherapy books related to children.

The aim of this particular collection of scripts is to promote a child's wellbeing and this is the recurring theme through all the scripts presented (fully acknowledging of course a hypnotherapist will need to work on a child's specific problems or difficulties as well). The scripts are written in a way to focus on the key issues so prevalent in our society today (e.g. anxiety, lack of confidence, low self-esteem or self-image as a result of experiencing bullying, neglect or abuse) which must be addressed in order to promote a child's wellbeing.

Who the book is for

I have always really enjoyed writing scripts for my clients (both children and adults) but I am aware that some hypnotherapists do not feel confident in writing scripts themselves. I am equally aware that students and newly qualified hypnotherapists can find scripts useful, as starting out on a new career can be very scary and it takes times to build confidence in one's own practice. Having a prepared script to hand can help with this. Experienced hypnotherapists who like using scripts will also find this collection useful. A hypnotherapist does not have to stick rigidly to a script because they need to go with where the client takes them. A good hypnotherapist will always adapt a script to meet the needs of their individual client. Many of the scripts are Ericksonian[1] in style in that they tell a story and can be used as a metaphor.

How the book came into being

A few years ago, I moved into a new practice location, which was located by the side of a river, and I am still there now. The therapy room is actually located on an island in the middle of a city. I am very lucky in that the therapy room window looks out onto the river and I have the riverbank right outside my window and door. As soon as

I moved in, I became aware of all the different animals that live, work and play in and around the river. Immediately I got lots of ideas for scripts from drifting off into trance myself whilst looking out of the window.

The children who first came to the new practice location loved the animals they saw before they came into the therapy room. Many of them imagined more things related to the river and the animals once they went into trance; this came very naturally as they just allowed things to happen. All this inspired me to start writing scripts specifically related to what the children imagined regarding the animals, the river and surrounding area. I thought it would be helpful to put some of these scripts together in a book for those students who are training to be a hypnotherapist, for newly qualified hypnotherapists and also established hypnotherapists. I have also included scripts I have written and used frequently for children I have worked with in other settings (e.g. schools and colleges).

My background

I have always worked with both children and adults; first as a social worker and then as both a social worker and clinical hypnotherapist, which I think is a good combination. My specialism has always been working with abuse issues. Survivors of abuse need help with the short and long-term effects of their abusive experiences. In my social work career I have always practised in a psychodynamic way. I believe that it is necessary to find the root cause of a problem and work on that before a person can move forward, rather than just focussing on the here and now. I work in the same way in my hypnotherapy practice and hence why I favour using regression techniques when appropriate; I believe this can be done with even a young child – depending on their development and maturity. Promoting the wellbeing of a survivor of any form of abuse is of paramount importance as very often their mental health has been affected. I enjoy undertaking this work both on a one-to-one basis but also in groups.

This book is primarily for working with children, although I have on occasion adapted some of the scripts for adults. I see children in two practice locations situated in two different cities, in schools and colleges and I also do home visits. I am a trained Hypnotherapy in Schools Programme (HISP) Practitioner[2] so I go into schools and colleges to facilitate groups to help with exam anxiety; I also work with a wide range of difficulties on an individual basis in those settings. In this book I have included some scripts which have been developed when working with specific exam anxiety groups.

So who is a child?

In my own practice I work with children from the age of 5 years upwards. A child in the UK is deemed to be anyone less than 18 years of age. A lot of 16 to 17 year olds present as mature young people and are very 'adult'. I have never been into saying a script is for a particular age group. Some scripts will obviously suit a younger child better, but many abused children have 'lost' or 'never had' their childhoods so it can be appropriate to use those scripts in certain circumstances. Best practice is to find out what the child's interests are and find or write an appropriate script.

In this book I have not stated any specific age group for the individual scripts. I believe that a hypnotherapist will be able to adapt the language to make it age appropriate for their client. I have used the term '*special mind*' in the scripts. Again, the hypnotherapist may choose to use an alternative term that suits the child better.

In the text I have used the word '*child*' throughout for simplicity rather than repeating child and young person. Therefore, my use of '*child*' includes anyone from the age of five to seventeen years old.

Wellbeing and mental health

It has already been stated above that the main objective (and theme) of this collection of scripts is to promote a child's wellbeing but what is '*wellbeing*' exactly? It will mean something different to every individual child or adult. Many dictionary definitions focus on health and happiness:

- The state of being comfortable, healthy or happy (Oxford English Dictionary)
- The state of feeling healthy and happy (Cambridge English Dictionary)
- A good or satisfactory condition of existence; a state characterized by health, happiness and prosperity (Dictionary.com)

I find this interesting because I have always thought it is important to ask all my clients (as a hypnotherapist and a social worker) the question 'What makes you happy?' I believe striving to be happy, content and satisfied with your life is of paramount importance and a starting point for planning work/treatment and setting goals.

Promoting the wellbeing of both children and adults is being given more and more attention nowadays as awareness is increasing around mental health (particularly in regard to children and even very young children), which the World Health Organisation has defined as:

- a state of wellbeing in which every individual realizes his or her own potential, can cope with the normal stresses of life, can work productively and fruitfully, and is able to make a contribution to his or her community.[3]

Certainly, anxiety is a key issue for many children nowadays and in my own hypnotherapy practice in recent years I have seen an increase in the number of referrals for anxiety – general, social and exam. Therefore, it is vital that a hypnotherapist finds out what work needs to be undertaken in order for a child to feel happy and for them to regard their life as going well, and that they are progressing and succeeding in what they want to do and achieve.

Although this book is concerned with children, I think it would be helpful to briefly mention the fact that the *Care Act 2014* (which relates to adults) introduced a definition of wellbeing which included the following nine aspects[4]:

- Personal dignity (including treatment of the individual with respect)
- Physical and mental health and emotional wellbeing
- Protection from abuse and harm
- Control by the individual over day-to-day life (including over care and support provided and the way it is provided)
- Participation in work, education, training or recreation

- Social and economic wellbeing
- Domestic, family and personal relationships
- Suitability of living accommodation
- The individual's contribution to society.

I think these aspects can be useful (especially when working with 16 and 17 year olds) but definitely need to be broken down further in order to be meaningful and effective. For example, I feel strongly that physical and mental health should be separated out as they are very different aspects of one's health. The same can be said for social and economic factors; they are very different aspects of one's life. Relationships could also be extended i.e. be much more specific – especially for those young people who have apprenticeships or are in employment. I find when assessing a child's wellbeing it is helpful to spend time talking about who is important to the child and what relationships they have in their life and also ones they would like to have.

Other aspects of wellbeing which have been included in assessments historically have been:

- Values
- Beliefs
- Culture
- Services
- Equipment
- Leisure/hobbies/interests
- Education
- Employment
- Transport
- History/memories
- Ambitions
- Death/dying.

I think going back to basics is always helpful and I frequently return to the work of Abraham Maslow[5] and his hierarchy of needs for lots of reasons. I believe Maslow's theory can help us focus on wellbeing too if we ask what a child's needs are, remembering that needs can be both physical and emotional. Maslow's hierarchy of needs was divided into:

Physiological: food; water; clothing; shelter
Safety: security; protection; safety; freedom from fear
Belongingness: connection to others; giving and receiving love; belonging; being accepted
Esteem: self-respect; esteem of others; self-confidence; worth
Self-actualisation: develop own capabilities; reaching full potential.

It is essential to undertake a thorough assessment before starting hypnosis with a child and it is helpful to also include assessing a child's wellbeing as part of the process. In the book I have included a script to facilitate this (Lily Lavender's Wellbeing Shop) and have included appendices to explain how to undertake an assessment of wellbeing and an assessment form, which can be used in the conscious state or the trance state.

Although technology can be a very positive thing and developments have aided us all immensely, a concern of mine is how children can become addicted to devices and ultimately can become isolated. Social media does connect people, which can be a good thing, but we are all aware that there can be negatives as well (e.g. cyberbullying). I find an increasing number of children are telling me that they spend a lot of time in their bedrooms communicating on their devices rather than socialising face-to-face. It becomes a habit to be constantly checking for text messages, e-mails, photos and so on. This activity often continues into the early hours of the morning (especially if parents/carers are not monitoring what their child is doing). So children can become 'hyper' in the sense that they cannot slow down and relax. Children need to be encouraged to use their imaginations rather than become solely dependent on the internet and electronic devices for entertainment. Choosing to go into trance to relax and taking time out on a regular basis is an alternative and healthier way of life for a child and will promote their wellbeing.

I emphasise throughout the book that a proper, thorough assessment is absolutely crucial, in order to decide how best to work with a child and develop an effective treatment plan. There are so many different techniques that can be used in hypnotherapy and a hypnotherapist will have their own preferences, but the hypnotherapist must always use what is best for the child. When working with children some hypnotherapists favour the solution-focussed approach and some are very much against using regression techniques. So in the book the hypnotherapist will find scripts which include the following:

- Ericksonian approach/metaphors/story-telling
- Solution-focussed approach
- Benefits approach
- Parts therapy
- Gestalt therapy
- Regression therapy.

Hypnotherapy is about unlearning, getting rid of things that hinder a child's wellbeing and making changes to ultimately promote a child's wellbeing. It is all about working on thoughts, feelings and behaviours. The purpose of the book is to offer ways of *how* to do this. The scripts present alternative ways of undertaking this work depending on a child's interests.

Notes

1. Milton Erickson was an American psychiatrist whose approach to hypnosis involved the use of indirect suggestion, metaphor and storytelling.
2. For more information about the Hypnotherapy in Schools Programme (HISP) visit: http://www.hypnotherapyinschools.co.uk.
3. https://www.who.int/mental_health/who_urges_investment/en/
4. pp.1–2, Department of Health (2014) *Care and Support Statutory Guidance.*
5. Original writings: Maslow. A. (1943) 'A Theory of Human Motivation', *Psychological Review* 50(4), 370–396; Maslow, A. (1954) *Motivation and Personality.* New York: Harper. These works are now available as modern publications.

Chapter 2

How to use the scripts

Having written this book it is obvious that I think that scripts have a place in the life of a working hypnotherapist. There has been much debate in the past (and I am sure the debates will continue) about whether a hypnotherapist should use scripts or whether it is better to be intuitive. I personally feel there is room for both. It is all dependent on the client (child or adult) and their needs, which are of paramount importance, and also what the hypnotherapist feels comfortable with in regard to their working practices. Other important factors to consider are how experienced the hypnotherapist is and how confident they are in their work.

As explained in the introduction, this book is aimed at students, newly qualified and experienced hypnotherapists. A reputable hypnotherapy training school will have spent time going through how to use and deliver scripts. However, I think before using the scripts in this book the reader may find it helpful to revisit some of the basic things any hypnotherapist should think about when deciding whether to use a script and then how to deliver it. After which I shall say more about using the scripts presented in this book.

Do I need a script?

Some fundamental questions a hypnotherapist might ask themselves are:

Do I want to use a script?
Do I need to use a script?
What is the script going to achieve?

Students and newly qualified hypnotherapists may feel a script will aid and support them when they are in the early stages of their development/career. They may be doubting themselves or lacking in confidence as they start putting what they have learnt through training into practice. Also, someone who has always worked with adults may experience some nervousness when starting to work with children. A script can feel a bit like a safety blanket – in a positive, supportive way.

A more experienced hypnotherapist may feel that they need something new and fresh to stimulate their work and ideas. A busy hypnotherapist may say they do not have time to write new scripts for every child. Some hypnotherapists just do not enjoy writing a script themselves.

It is important for the hypnotherapist to ask themselves a number of questions when considering using a script with a child. These questions should be in the hypnotherapist's mind when undertaking the assessment (and answered in full by the time the assessment has been completed) because it is vital to find the right way of working with each individual child. During the assessment the hypnotherapist will have gained in-depth information about the child and the presenting problem(s); after which the best way of working with the child should be clear and an appropriate treatment plan developed.

When considering whether to use a script in a therapy session the hypnotherapist needs to focus on the following:

- The best way of working with the child i.e. what is right for him/her
- Methods/techniques which might prove to be useful
- Important/significant people in the child's life; role models
- Favourite characters (in books; on television; in films; in games); heroes/heroines
- Interests/hobbies/activities (to identify which scripts may engage the child)
- Likes/dislikes
- Fears/phobias the child may have (so certain scripts might be avoided e.g. if the child does not like animals)
- When and how to use the script in a session
- Whether the script will be the main/only method to be used in the trance part of the session or will other methods be introduced for the therapeutic work planned for that particular session.
- Whether music will be used in the session. It can be useful to use a piece of music in an actual therapy session (and subsequent sessions) and then use the same music when making a CD/MP3 file for the child to use at home. The music is like an anchor i.e. when hearing the music in the future it reinforces what has been learnt or embedded in the hypnotherapy session.

Preparation

A hypnotherapist needs to find a script in the first instance and then become familiar with it by reading it over and over. This takes time and the hypnotherapist should never underestimate the amount of time that might be needed for preparation. Thorough preparation is the key to delivering a script in an effective way. Scripts can be written in many different styles and formats. The hypnotherapist should feel comfortable with the style and language used but I also feel it is important that the hypnotherapist adapts a script to meet the needs of the child and themselves. For example, some writers of scripts include pause marks or use bold for emphasis. I believe if there is going to be interaction between the hypnotherapist and the child (i.e. the script is not purely going to be read as a story/metaphor), the hypnotherapist should follow the pace of the child and introduce their own pauses and emphases. If a script is followed rigidly, there is a danger the hypnotherapist sounds unnatural and maybe robotic.

If the hypnotherapist is going to just read a script straight through, then it is imperative that they do not sound like they are reading. Whatever is being said needs to sound interesting and meaningful; intonation in the voice is vital. So rehearsal is important – especially for people who are training to be a hypnotherapist or who are newly qualified.

There should be lots of rehearsal whilst training to become a hypnotherapist, but I think we all need to keep practising because we never stop learning about how we present ourselves; we can learn from experience and the mistakes we make. The reality is we all have off days (perhaps because we are feeling ill but do not cancel a session because we do not want to let the client down) when we might not be practising at our best.

It is a good idea to record oneself during a rehearsal, either using a small dictaphone or the recording facility on a mobile phone. It is vital to listen to oneself over and over and learn from what we hear.

The stages of preparation can be summarised as follows:

- Become familiar with the script by reading it over and over.
- Adapt the script (if required) to meet the child's needs. Change the content or language to make the script age appropriate. Some of the scripts in this book are obviously not suitable for certain age groups. In the main I have not stated an appropriate age group for a script. However, many scripts could be used for a wide age range if the language is adapted – hence the need for preparation.
- Start rehearsals using the script, incorporating the adaptations and make further changes as necessary (these will become obvious with practice).
- Think about using and including your own direct/indirect statements, suggestions and the commands which need to be embedded. This is particularly important when using some of the scripts in this book as I have suggested in parts that the hypnotherapist might wish to undertake more in-depth work with the child i.e. the script only forms part of the session.
- More rehearsal: at this stage make a note of how long it takes to get through the script. An essential part of preparation is allowing enough time for a session. A session should never be rushed nor should the child be brought out of trance very quickly because time is running out. Some hypnotherapists hire rooms for their sessions and in a busy practice centre they may have to be out of a room on the dot – there is no flexibility to allow for running over time. It is wise to book an extra 15 minutes to avoid being rushed. It is also important to leave enough time between clients to reflect on the last client and prepare for the next one.

Using your voice

Using a script is not like reading a story to a child. You have to make it your own by sounding natural and as already stated above, the hypnotherapist should not sound like they are actually reading from a script. The hypnotherapist needs to think about and constantly evaluate their own use of:

Soft voice

Every hypnotherapist will have developed their own 'hypnotherapy voice', which should be soft but also clear and loud enough for the child to hear. There may be an inclination to be too quiet when trying to present the voice in a soft way. Thinking about the intonation of one's voice i.e. the rise and fall, should help with the soft presentation. The listeners (the child and the subconscious) are more likely to pay attention if the voice is interesting; a script should not be delivered in a flat or monotone voice. The hypnotherapist needs to think about tone, pitch and emphasis.

Tone

The tone of voice indicates the way you feel about something. The hypnotherapist should be aware of their own feelings during the session and ensure that they are not expressed in the tone of their voice (i.e. not to present surprise, shock, horror, anger, sadness, amusement or disbelief).

Pitch

Pitch can be low or high, and again can be affected by how the hypnotherapist is feeling. So when a student or newly qualified hypnotherapist feels a little bit nervous their voice could become high-pitched; they might even stutter or hesitate.

Emphasis

In order to be clear and make a point, the hypnotherapist should put emphasis on certain words and phrases within a script. As I have already said, I prefer a hypnotherapist to put their own interpretation into a script and hence why I have not used pause marks and only used italics for emphases occasionally in the scripts presented.

Pace

If a hypnotherapist is feeling a bit nervous due to using a script for the first time (or for any other reason), then there could be a tendency to speak too quickly. A good rule of thumb when using a script is to sound to yourself as though you are speaking slightly too slowly. You are then probably presenting at the right pace.

Pauses and silences

If the hypnotherapist proactively thinks about when to use pauses and silences within a script, it is going to help with making statements, giving suggestions and embedding commands when using a script. It will also help the hypnotherapist to keep going at a slow, unhurried pace. A pause when working with a child could be up to five seconds. A silence could be up to 20 seconds or longer. When rehearsing it is good to practise counting the seconds and differentiate between a pause and a silence.

Practical matters

The voice is not the only part of their body language that the hypnotherapist needs to think about. The hypnotherapist will have been trained to sit comfortably (not fidget) and adopt an open position in order to build rapport. The hypnotherapist will take notes during the assessment and may make further notes as the session proceeds. So keeping paper and script(s) in order and within easy access is vital to the process. The hypnotherapist needs to decide where they are going to hold the script and avoid the rustle of papers when the child is in trance.

The hypnotherapist also needs to think about the fact (especially if they have not worked with children before) that some children have their eyes open when in trance or they can suddenly come out of trance (and go back in just as quickly).

So it is important to give some thought to how the hypnotherapist will look to the child if they suddenly come back to the conscious state and see the hypnotherapist reading. Therefore, the positioning of paperwork (as well as oneself) should be considered.

Structuring the session

So far, the discussion has been focussing on how the hypnotherapist should prepare for using a script. Part of the preparation process should include thinking about the structure of the session, so I want to go back to basics again and state the obvious. A hypnotherapy session will usually be structured as follows:

- Welcome
- Building rapport
- Assessment in the conscious state (if the first session)
- Discussion and review in the conscious state (if a returning client) i.e. how things have gone since the last session
- Introduction to trance
- Deepener (if needed)
- Therapeutic work to be undertaken
- Trance termination
- Awakening
- Discussion in the conscious state.

A younger child (five to nine years of age) will have a shorter concentration span and therefore sessions will also be shorter – maybe 30 to 40 minutes. Certain conditions which affect concentration (e.g. attention deficit hyperactivity disorder (ADHD), chronic fatigue, general anxiety disorder), may also necessitate shorter sessions. Older children can engage for longer, so booking an hour is usually appropriate. I find some mature teenagers (15 years onwards) present as adults and on occasions I have run sessions for 75 or 90 minutes. The hypnotherapist never knows where the child and the subconscious are going to take him/her. So allowing enough time is vital and reinforces the discussion above, namely that the hypnotherapist should be able to estimate how long it is going to take to read a script straight through, or if there is to be interaction, how much time might be needed.

I want to stress how important it is to allocate time for bringing the child out of trance, what many call the 'awakening'. After doing the main therapeutic work, the hypnotherapist with the child should review what has been learnt, practise any new skills and reinforce any suggestions/commands before bringing the child gently back to the conscious state. However, some children will come out of trance as and when it suits them.

Scripts in the book

The scripts which follow can be used in a variety of ways to suit the needs of the hypnotherapist and the child they are working with. For some of the scripts it will be up to the hypnotherapist whether they use a script purely as a metaphor or whether they want to be more interactive with the child. Some of the scripts are written in a specific guided way and will be of particular use to the student or newly qualified hypnotherapist. I have included questions in some of the scripts which the hypnotherapist can use to do more in-depth work. The more experienced hypnotherapist may use a script as a starting point and then see where the child goes with it. This is the exciting thing about hypnosis; the hypnotherapist never knows where they are going to be taken and very often they have to think and react very quickly.

I have written an introduction to each script, some of which are very short because the script does not need any explanation – a properly qualified hypnotherapist will understand the intention. Other introductions are longer where I felt more explanation was needed. Following the introduction the hypnotherapist will find one or more main scripts. Shorter additional scripts follow some of the main scripts, which the hypnotherapist can choose to use or not (as they may prefer to use their own treatment techniques). Some questions have been included to be used as prompts if needed. I have included some guidance notes in the scripts but only when I have felt this is really necessary and these are marked clearly.

As already stated above, I have not included pause marks in the scripts. I have only occasionally put words into italics – my rationale being that I think a hypnotherapist will want to use their own emphasis.

I have not presented the scripts in order of problems, treatments or methods. The scripts cover the following subject areas:

- Introducing the child to trance
- Demonstrating the power of the imagination
- Deepeners
- Relaxation
- Using the imagination – going on journeys
- Focussing/concentration/distraction
- Changing thoughts, feelings and behaviours
- Lack of confidence; low self-esteem/self-worth
- Negative image
- Lack of motivation/determination
- Getting rid of things
- Being in control
- Anxiety: general, social and exam
- Fear, phobias, habits
- Learning and recalling information
- Sleep issues
- Bullying
- Abuse
- Bereavement and loss.

In order for the hypnotherapist to find their way around the book and find a useful script, I have included a summary of the content of each chapter in the following appendix.

12　How to use the scripts

Appendix 1: Summary of what the scripts cover

The summaries below are provided so that the reader is aware of what is covered in each chapter and hence make it easier to find an appropriate script for their work.

3. Just imagine

When meeting a child for the first time, a vital part of a hypnotherapist's work is to get to know the child and build rapport, whilst undertaking a full assessment. This is done initially by demonstrating the power of the imagination in a fun way to the child. The three scripts presented – 'Fancy dress show', 'The sandpit' and 'Bubbles'– offer ways of doing this and introduce the child to trance. Using one or more of the scripts will also enable the hypnotherapist to assess whether the child is visual, auditory, kinaesthetic, olfactory or gustatory. The third script also allows the hypnotherapist to help the child to create a safe place, which can be used in future sessions.

4. Travelling glow: Colour relaxation

The purpose of the script is to relax both the body and mind of the child. It gets the child to focus and concentrate on a colour, which forms a glow which will then move at a gentle, unhurried pace down the outside of the body and also on the inside. The relaxing glow continues to travel slowly as the child is encouraged to look at the colour and the different shades of dark and light. The child will go into trance as both the body and the mind become relaxed. The script can be used purely for relaxation purposes, but can also help with any sleeping problems a child might be experiencing.

5. Exploring the island in the city

The main purpose of the script is to get the child into trance by first exploring a city centre and then going to an island which exists within the city. The child is encouraged to use any way of moving in their imagination. When the island is reached the child is shown various places (the river, houses, workplaces, buildings, shops, and eateries) and explores the island further. Whilst using the script for relaxation purposes the hypnotherapist will also be able to assess the modalities i.e. whether the child is visual, auditory, kinaesthetic, olfactory or gustatory.

6. The flea market

To get a child into trance it can be useful to get them to focus on an object. Real objects can be used and given to the child when in the conscious state; the child is then helped to focus on the object. However, objects created in the imagination can be used instead of a tangible object and this script facilitates this. The script sets the child on a mission to find an object in the flea market which can be used to get him/her into trance before doing more in-depth work in the session. It can be used to encourage exploration and work on focus, concentration and play.

7. Relaxing on the riverbank: Having some quiet time

Children who are hyperactive or who have been diagnosed as being on the autistic spectrum or with attention deficit hyperactivity disorder (ADHD) or Asperger's syndrome need to learn to relax and have quiet time. The objective in using this script is to teach a child how to relax by imagining Desi the duck and her twelve ducklings having quiet time on the riverbank and then encouraging the child to imagine him/herself having quiet time with the ducks. The script can also be used with any child who finds it hard to wind down or who is experiencing sleeping difficulties; this may be due to spending too much time on their devices such as mobile phone and iPad.

8. Fire

The four scripts presented use fire as a powerful tool in the imagination. The first two scripts facilitate gentle relaxation to get the child into the trance state and then deepening. One script is set indoors and the other outdoors. The two additional scripts can be used to do more in-depth work and work particularly well with children who have experienced abuse. 'Burning stuff' encourages the child to get rid of memories or things they do not want (thoughts, feelings, behaviours) by throwing them on the fire and watching them burn. The fourth script uses fireworks and a rocket to go on a journey to either use regression or to forward pace. Ultimately, the journey can facilitate healing and promote the child's wellbeing.

9. The maze

A child can experience a whole gamut of emotions when they are in a low mood. The maze can be used to work on problems in relation to feeling confused, unable to make a decision, hopeless, trapped or no point to anything. Using the maze embeds the idea that it is alright to take your time to make a decision and that there is always a solution to every problem. The script begins with getting the child into trance by walking to and then entering the maze; exploring the maze gets the child into a deeper level of relaxation. There is then scope for the hypnotherapist to work on specific difficulties and blockages the child has. It is a script which can be returned to in future sessions.

10. The beards

This script is a deepener and is to be used once the child has gone into trance. By getting the child to focus on the beards of a father and a son and then taking a journey into the beards, the hypnotherapist will be able to get the child into a deeper level of relaxation in preparation for undertaking therapy in the rest of the session.

11. Traffic lights

Using a set of traffic lights is a very useful strategy which the child can put into practice immediately after the therapeutic session has taken place. Using the traffic lights can stop negative, intrusive or repetitive thoughts, but they can also be used to stop unwanted feelings or promote changes in behaviour or way of thinking. This is done by firstly focussing on the red light to stop thoughts or feelings. The child then focuses on the amber light to think about how they would like to think and feel in the future, and what needs to be done to achieve this. The green light gives them the message to go and put those things into action (forward pacing). The script can be used in one-to-one sessions or in group work e.g. exam anxiety groups.

12. The workshop

Sometimes a child will want to separate out the activities they have in their life e.g. work/study and fun things. This script creates a workshop for the child where s/he can work on the specific issue for which they are having hypnotherapy. The workshop can be used in future hypnotherapy sessions and the hypnotherapist will encourage the child to go back to the workshop in between the sessions to continue to work and practise the strategies they have learnt. The aim of the script is to create a workshop which has all sorts of things/equipment (anything the child needs) in it that can help with an issue. The workshop is a safe place in which to work on difficult thoughts, feelings and behaviours and where things can be left behind until the child feels ready to undertake more work and practice.

13. A bit of stomping

Mantras can be a useful way of reinforcing the work which has been undertaken in a hypnotherapy session. A child can develop a mantra when in trance and then use it in between sessions both in the conscious state and when in trance. This script is to be used at the end of a session in order to embed a mantra, but also to introduce some fun into the therapy being experienced. The idea of stomping has been developed from an exercise used on assertiveness training developed by the author. In the script the mantra 'I am confident' is used to encourage belief in self, motivation and determination. The child learns how to stomp out the mantra in a school hall or any other location the child may prefer.

14. The clock

The clock demonstrates to the child how they can take control and make things happen – in this case regarding the movement of time – making it go faster or slower. The script reinforces the knowledge and the belief that the subconscious mind can achieve anything you really want to do. This is a useful script to help a child make time go quicker when they are dreading something or wanting to get something over with very quickly e.g. a visit to the dentist; a hospital appointment; taking an exam; attending a funeral. Alternatively, it can be used to slow time down in order to relive a good memory from the past or to savour an experience which might occur in the future.

15. Going back in time

Two scripts are presented to facilitate the regression of a child. The scripts will enable a hypnotherapist to find the root cause of a problem and then release the emotions which are attached to the incident or experiences(s). The first script uses a castle's drawbridge to get the child into trance and then the inside of the castle is used to regress the child to earlier times – even a past life. The second script uses a steam train to travel back in time. The child sits in a carriage and watches their life go backwards outside the window. The train slows down and then stops at a time in the child's life or a specific incident that needs to be worked on. The child is given the choice as to whether they want to get off the train and be in the centre of their past or whether they want to watch from afar i.e. through the window.

16. Star in the sky

The main script takes the child on a journey to find their very own star, which can become their safe place if they want it to be. The journey takes the child into trance and deepens them. Three additional scripts follow which all have different purposes and should be used after the main script has got the child into trance. 'Exploring the moon' is good to use in a first session to demonstrate how the imagination can take the child to different places to explore and find things. 'Swinging to sleep' is for children who have difficulty getting to sleep and/or they wake up frequently in the night. The script gives them a technique of getting to sleep or back to sleep. 'Looking for the spiritual star' is for bereaved children, who are struggling with the loss of a person or who may be too young to understand the concept of death. The script helps them find the star of the person who has died and offers the opportunity to talk to the person.

17. Harry the heron

Harry the heron introduces the concept of stillness. Introducing Harry to a child who is hyperactive or who finds it difficult to concentrate is a way of encouraging relaxation. The script introduces Harry and then encourages the child to imagine that s/he is a heron. The child takes a journey and learns how to control at what speed they fly and where they go. Then the child is encouraged to unwind and relax each part of the body whilst standing in the river. These are learning strategies which can be used in the future to feel calm and still.

18. Bertie the beagle

A lot of children who get overexcited will be able to relate to the story of Bertie the beagle, who was very mischievous when he was a puppy and got told off a lot. The script introduces the 'Benefits Approach' in hypnotherapy, which is often used for adults but is also effective when working with children whose behaviour is considered to be problematic by others. Helen the hypnotherapist, who works with human beings and animals, hears that the owners of Bertie are having some problems with his behaviour. She volunteers to take Bertie for a few walks and then teaches him number breathing and an anchor word 'calm'. So very quickly he learns how to be calm and also respectful of others, who may be affected by his behaviour.

19. Chinga the cat

Chinga the cat has a fear of needles due to a previous bad experience at the vet's when she was a kitten. She goes to visit Helen the hypnotherapist who helps her with her fear by teaching her relaxation techniques and creating a safe place. Helen then uses a regression technique to take Chinga back to the original bad experience and releases the feelings attached to the memory. Forward pacing is then used to help Chinga prepare for her future operation. This script can be used to deal with other fears and phobias a child may be experiencing.

20. The salmon triplets

Some children scratch because they have a condition like eczema; others just scratch out of habit. Itching and scratching can often be related to stress and anxiety. The salmon triplets had a condition which caused their skin and scales to be itchy and uncomfortable. The script is metaphorical and illustrates how remedies can be created in the imagination and habits can be stopped with the help of anchors created whilst in the trance state. The salmon triplets meet an older salmon, Samuel, who had had the same condition as themselves when he was younger. Samuel gets the triplets into trance and takes them to meet Danny the dolphin, who swims with them to a part of the sea with healing powers and where they find seaweed which is used as an anchor.

21. Maurice the mole

The story of Maurice the mole is aimed at children who are seen as 'loners' and maybe considered to be a bit 'odd' because they enjoy solitude. It can also be used for children who have become isolated through bullying, being ridiculed or mocked for whatever reason. One of the key messages in the script is that people can make assumptions about a person (i.e. how they look and how they behave) which are totally incorrect. One winter when the snow comes down Maurice gets trapped in a tunnel he is digging. He becomes panicky and frightened. He distracts himself by using breathing exercises and mantras, and using a resource which is unique to him – his snout – which others had made fun of before saying it was far too long.

22. Harriet the hedgehog

The central subject being addressed in this script is bullying. In society today bullying can be carried out in so many different ways – face-to-face, using devices, using the internet – which can ultimately affect many aspects of a child's life. Harriet the hedgehog was rejected by her mother and bullied by her siblings. Harriet's leg had been permanently damaged during her birth and consequently she walked with a limp. She remembers words and phrases that were said to her, which resulted in her low self-esteem, lack of confidence and mistrust of people. Children who have been abused or who have a disability will benefit from hearing about Harriet's experiences; how she worked on getting rid of the negative words/phrases which had stayed with her; how she overcame her self-doubt and how eventually she started a new life with animals she could trust.

23. Bees in the hives

Parts Therapy is a very effective method of resolving issues when inner conflict exists. It can work well with children, but needs to be kept simple, especially if there is more than one part in the subconscious that are pulling in different directions. The script is metaphorical in that it suggests a beehive and its honeycombs are like parts of the child's mind. Using the bees in the hive the hypnotherapist will be able to work with the child to make changes and resolve conflict. This will be done by using the bees already working in the hives i.e. certain parts of the child's subconscious; finding out whether some bees need to retire and whether other bees (parts) need to be brought in. In some cases the working bees and new bees may agree to work in the hive together.

24. Butterflies passing by

Dealing with bereavement, grieving and encouraging remembrance and commemoration are the main objectives of these scripts. The main script introduces the idea of butterflies being passing souls in transition. The child is encouraged to fly with the butterflies and find the person who has died. The script offers the opportunity for the child to vent their feelings, ask any questions they may have and spend time with the person. Children may have lost someone very close to them or it could be someone not so close but still affects them (e.g. a fellow student who has committed suicide). When a death has been sudden and maybe unexpected there can be many unresolved issues. Two additional scripts are included so more in-depth work can be undertaken regarding the grieving process. 'Remembering and commemorating' can help with anniversary blues i.e. when a child consciously or subconsciously feels low on a specific date or a certain time of year. The third script presents a letter written by Rex the rat who never knew his parents, because they died in an accident and he needs to say how he feels. The child is then encouraged to write their own letter.

25. Lily Lavender's Wellbeing Shop

Lily Lavender is a great role model for children of all ages who struggle with learning and who do not believe they can succeed. The main script tells the story of Lily, who was diagnosed with dyslexia when at school. Lily became interested in alternative therapies, experimenting and doing things differently. She worked hard and was determined to succeed. She became a beautician and eventually achieved her ambition of opening a wellbeing shop. The main script takes the child into Lily's shop to see all the things she sells and where Lily works in her wellbeing room. The additional script 'The relaxing candle wax' is an introduction to trance, and is a deepener. The purpose of 'Wash it away' is to get rid of a thought, feeling or behaviour. 'Bottle of confidence' builds self-esteem, but confidence can also be replaced with something else in the bottle e.g. motivation, determination. Appendix 1 explains how to undertake a wellbeing assessment using the form which is in Appendix 2. The assessment and form can be used in the conscious state or when the child is in trance. If the child is going to attend for several sessions it can be used to review and grade their wellbeing at the beginning of each session.

26. The Fairy House

The emphasis in this script is for the child to think about having a healthy, happy life and promoting wellbeing. Through talking about fairies and the work they do, messages are embedded about healthy living, food and growing in different ways – physically and emotionally; growing in strength and confidence. The script also introduces the idea of healing and protection. The fairies give the child two anchors – a magic wand and fairy dust. They then make suggestions on how the wand and dust may be used to help with changing feelings, growing, mending or healing.

27. Getting rid of stuff at the business centre

This script has a broad use as its theme is one of disposal. Therefore, it can be used to get rid of many unhelpful things for the child – thought, feeling, behaviour, a specific memory, fear, phobia or habit. Gestalt methodology underpins this script by getting the child to visualise what they want to get rid of and boxing it up before getting rid of it at the business centre. The child explores the centre and finds lots of different places and things which will help with the disposal. The child is encouraged to talk about the disposal and the related feelings of release.

28. The post office

The main objective of taking the child to the post office is to get rid of things. The scripts were originally written for children who had been abused but can also be used for children who have been bullied or bereaved. The child finds things in the post office which enables them to express themselves in different ways (e.g. through drawing, painting or writing) if they usually find it difficult to talk about things verbally in the conscious state. Another objective is that the child can get rid of unwanted thoughts, feelings and fears associated with a memory. This is facilitated by using the additional scripts: 'Draw or paint a picture' or 'Writing a letter' using the facilities of the post office. 'Posting a parcel' is offered to get rid of whatever needs to go. The final script 'Invisible bubble wrap' is for promoting protection and the feeling of safety.

29. The art gallery

The main script tells the story of Leah and Malik, who were struggling artists but now run the art gallery. Both artists had troubled childhoods experiencing bullying, abuse, issues around sexuality and disability and discrimination. The story explains some of the long-term effects of their experiences – lack of self-belief, negative self-image and an eating disorder. Leah and Malik eventually both achieve their ambition to be successful artists and want to help other people in their local community by opening the art gallery. Three additional scripts follow which can be used to work on specific problems. 'Self-portrait' works on image, how the child sees him/herself now and how they want to be in the future. 'An exhibition – The life of...' is a way of using regression and then working with the child to get rid of images, feelings, memories and then works on the future. 'Painting the walls' is specifically for use with children who have been bullied. Very often a child will have experienced name-calling or been accused of being something they have come to believe to be true. This script helps to get rid of the names, word and phrases.

30. The bakery

The kitchen within the bakery is a place where the child can work on a problem and find a solution by cooking with food ingredients but then adding special ingredients.

The child is very much in control and whilst in trance the subconscious will identify what needs to be done in order to resolve a problem. The script is very solution-focussed. This script also works well for working specifically on wellbeing. The child finds the special ingredients they need to improve how they live life now and what they want for the future. The main script introduces the child to the bakery and then an additional script 'Baking a banana cake' is included to illustrate how the hypnotherapist can take the child forward.

31. The climbing wall

At times a child may not know what to do about a certain situation or they may have a specific problem/dilemma or they are feeling very indecisive because they do not know in which direction they want their life to go. Indecision and uncertainty can cause fear and anxiety. The climbing wall can be used to help a child set one or more realistic goals and it gives them time to think how they are going to achieve what they want. There is a recurring theme through the script that there is no pressure or rush to make a decision; it is OK to take your time to decide what you want to achieve. Once the goals have been set the child climbs the wall; the child learns that there are different routes and pathways to be taken. The hypnotherapist and child can return to the climbing wall in future sessions. The script can also be used to focus solely on a child's wellbeing. Work can be undertaken to identify what would make the child happy and how this can be achieved with motivation and determination.

32. Bennett's Bicycle Shop

The main script tells the story of Arlo who visits Mr Bennett's Bicycle Shop on the pretence that there is something wrong with his bicycle's brakes. Arlo actually wants to talk about how he finds writing difficult and he dreads the spelling tests he has every Monday morning, so much so he feels sick and cannot eat from Sunday night. Mr Bennett teaches Arlo a technique to get rid of the 'horrible feelings' by imagining letting air out of the bicycle's tyres and then pumping fresh new air into the tyres. There are many children who struggle with different aspects of learning and even though they work hard, they fear that they are not going to be able to recall the information they have learnt. Although the main script is aimed at children of all ages who struggle with academic learning, it can also help children who may have to perform or succeed in other situations e.g. dancing in a show; singing solo; taking a driving test. An additional script is also included – 'Going for a ride' – which can be used to get a child into trance and to illustrate the power of the imagination by getting the bicycle to move in different ways.

33. Storing and recalling

Children can get scared or become anxious that they will forget how to do something (e.g. the steps in a dance) or they will not be able to recall an important piece of information (e.g. in an exam situation). The two main scripts aim to embed the understanding that the subconscious/special mind stores everything that has been heard, seen, said, read, learnt or done. The library and archives are metaphors for the subconscious mind but help the child to organise particular information in a way which is best for them. The scripts are useful for the child who experiences difficulty with learning, recalling information or exam anxiety. An additional script is included which can be used as a follow-on or stand-alone for a child who likes books. It includes a method of getting a message from the subconscious mind and also a regression technique which can be used to recall a particular incident which needs to be worked on. It is particularly useful for a child who has been abused and needs to go through the healing process.

34. The spa

The spa is a script which was originally written for an exam anxiety group, who were experiencing panic attacks which caused them to become very hot and sweaty. The spa has a sauna, steam room and a mountain of crushed ice which can lower the child's body temperature to the perfect state. The spa has other facilities too which can help with releasing and leaving things behind (in the swimming pool) and looking to the future i.e. forward pacing (whilst relaxing in the lounge and watching the large television screen). The receptionist in the spa takes the child on a tour of the spa to view (and use) the facilities which might help them with anxiety, physical symptoms manifesting from panic attacks and getting rid of specific problems, thoughts, feelings and memories.

35. The igloo

A child's body temperature can be affected when they are experiencing general or social anxiety or having a panic attack. The script was originally written for students in an exam anxiety group who became hot and sweaty whenever they thought about the revision they needed to do or when they were actually taking mock or real exams. Other children can become very cold and experience severe shivering when they are anxious. The igloo teaches the child how they can control their body temperature in different situations (not just exams) where they experience fear or anxiety. The walk taken to the igloo is also an effective way to get the child deeper into trance and into a more relaxed and calmer state before altering their body temperature.

36. Spencer the singer-songwriter

This metaphorical script tells the story of Spencer (age: 49 years) who witnessed his mother being harmed by her new partner after his dad left, and who was psychologically abused himself by the man he called 'the intruder'. Spencer developed many negative beliefs about himself and did not ever think he was 'good enough', especially in relation to wanting to be a professional singer and songwriter. Spencer was a very caring person but he also experienced a lot of anger – especially towards his mother who he felt had not protected him or his brothers. The script tells how Spencer does eventually build his self-esteem and confidence by believing in himself and that it is never too late to succeed. He also learns to accept compliments and build trust. Spencer performs his first solo gig in public using breathing techniques and using the first line of one of his songs as a mantra: 'Believe – don't let the past hold you back'.

Chapter 3

Just imagine

Introduction

All hypnotherapists know how important it is to build rapport with any client before undertaking any trance work with them. It is usually an absolute delight to work with children because they have such vivid imaginations and often little constraints – obviously depending on their age, personal experiences and circumstances. When getting to know a child and in order to build rapport the hypnotherapist will gain information about their interests, hobbies, heroes/heroines, favourite characters, which can then be used for therapeutic purposes.

An important stage of building a good therapeutic relationship is to demonstrate to the child in a fun way how powerful and clever their special mind/imagination is. In the first session it is essential that sufficient time is spent doing this to introduce the child to trance but also to lay the foundations for future sessions. What follows are three scripts I use with children to demonstrate the power of the imagination. Script 3 has an additional purpose as it can be used to create a safe place for the child to use immediately and in future sessions.

The first session can be a mixture of talking and doing 'fun' things in the trance state. It can be helpful for children who have shorter concentration spans to come in and out of trance during this introductory session. Children usually enjoy the different experiences each time and find it easy to go from the conscious state to the hypnotic state. Therefore, more than one script can be used if required. It is important for the hypnotherapist to ask the child about what they experienced and how they felt when they come out of trance.

Whilst using these scripts, the hypnotherapist will gain important insights which will inform the initial assessment. Gaining information about the child's senses is essential i.e. whether they are visual, auditory, kinaesthetic, olfactory or gustatory. This will also help the hypnotherapist to decide the best way of working with the child in future sessions.

Script 1: Fancy dress show

Every year there is a Summer Festival which runs for three days over a weekend. One of the events that happens every year is the fancy dress show for animals. It is the chance for any creature who wants to get dressed up to wear whatever they like.

Now I wonder if you can close your eyes and imagine some of the animals that live nearby. Start thinking about the different types of mammals, birds, fish and reptiles there may be. Then imagine one or maybe a few more animals – it is up to you – who you want to take part in the fancy dress show.

So imagine that the animals are lining up outside the changing rooms. They look just like they do every day. Imagine them going into the changing rooms. On the count of 3 they will come out of the changing rooms all dressed up – 1, 2, and 3.

Now see how the animals are dressed up ready in their costumes.
Tell me which animals you see.
What are the animals wearing?

(Guidance note: if the hypnotherapist wants a longer demonstration use the following)

Three animals have now reached the final of the fancy dress show.
Which three animals do you see?
What are they wearing?
Now in the final the animals have to sing, dance or do both.
What does Animal 1 do?
What does Animal 2 do?
What does Animal 3 do?
Did you hear any music when the animals were singing/dancing?
Who would you choose as the winner?
Tell the animals to start walking back to the changing rooms.
Now make the animals disappear completely.

Script 2: The sandpit

Imagine that you are sitting in a sandpit in a park. Unfortunately, the sandpit has not got much sand in it. That's not very good when you would like to build a sandcastle, is it?

As you look around you notice on one side of you there is a bucket and on the other side of you there is a spade.
Look at the bucket – tell me what colour it is.
What is it made of?
Now look at the spade – tell me what colour it is.
What is it made of?
Stretch both arms out in front of you with the palms of your hands turned upwards. That's right – good.

The bucket starts moving towards one of your hands and then it places itself on that hand. Keep both your arms stretched out – that's right – good.

Suddenly you become aware that the spade is starting to move. You see that a wizard (*or insert favourite character or hero/heroine of the child*) is holding the spade. The wizard (*or character*) says a few magic words and the spade starts moving upwards off the ground and going higher and higher until it is hovering directly over the bucket. The wizard says a few more magic words then suddenly sand starts pouring off the spade and goes down into the bucket. As you watch the sand pouring into the bucket it starts to pour quicker and quicker.

The bucket starts to fill up with sand. The wizard says a few more magic words and a lot more sand starts to pour into the bucket, which is getting heavier and heavier. The sand is pouring thick and fast now. There is just so much sand falling down from the spade into the bucket. The bucket is almost halfway full – have a look in.

It would be good to have the bucket full to the top, wouldn't it? So ask the wizard for more sand. The wizard says a few more magic words and suddenly – WHOOSH – a whole heap of sand begins to fall even faster and faster. The sand is rising in the bucket – it is almost three quarters full. Getting nearer and nearer the top. The bucket is SO heavy now; it is very difficult to hold it up. The sand has nearly reached to the top of the bucket…and then it does and it starts spilling over the sides into the sandpit.

You can keep filling the bucket with sand so you can go and build as many sand-castles as you like…

Script 3: Bubbles

Close your eyes and imagine that in front you there is a small tub full of liquid which can make bubbles. You also see a bubble blower, which you can hold in your hand. Pick up the bubble blower and dip it into the liquid – now blow.

See all the beautiful bubbles flying up and up. Some bubbles will be very small – others will be really big. As you look at all the bubbles you will see there are so many different sizes. You might see lots of different colours in the bubbles too. The bubbles are light and airy – and you can see right through them.

Now I want you to use your special mind to make some changes to the bubbles.

First of all, tell some of the bubbles to come next to each – tell them to get into a straight line.

Now make all those see-through, light and airy bubbles in the line turn solid and heavy.

Now make them change colour: black – white – blue – purple – red – green – orange.

Now make them all turn yellow – so they look like a line of tennis balls. Imagine you have a tennis racquet in your hand. Hit all the tennis balls far away so none are left.

Pick up the bubble blower again and blow some more bubbles. Watch them float up and up. They are so very light and airy. Look at the different sizes and all the different colours. So very pretty. It must be lovely to just float and float – just going anywhere. That must be very exciting as well.

Keep watching all the bubbles – there are so many of them. When you are ready – jump into one of the bubbles. The bubble is safe and strong – it won't burst. It is ready to carry you to anywhere you want to go.

It would be good to float to somewhere where you feel very safe, peaceful and happy. So just let the bubble float you away to that safe place. Go there now. Tell me when you get there.

Chapter 4

Travelling glow
Colour relaxation

Introduction

This script works for children of all ages and is a great way of relaxing both the body and the mind. I have found that teenagers in particular seem to enjoy this script. I regularly use it as an introduction in exam anxiety groups and have frequently found that group members want it to be used again at the beginning of other sessions.

For work with individuals, this is a good script to use to help the child relax after talking about breathing (and maybe doing some breathing exercises). It introduces them to trance very gently and gets them to a deeper level before doing more in-depth work in the session. It also demonstrates through the use of colours that they can change anything they want. The positive colour identified can also be used as an anchor in future work.

As the focus is on relaxation the script can be used solely for this purpose, but I have also found it very useful in helping a child who is experiencing problems getting to sleep. Instead of suggesting the child looks at the sun in the sky, the hypnotherapist should suggest s/he looks at the moon in the sky.

For younger children (c. five to eight year olds) some of the language should be changed (e.g. replacing 'stomach' with 'tummy'); and some things can be left out that would not be familiar to them (e.g. certain parts of the body, such as the intestine).

The script

Just imagine that you are lying on your back – somewhere outdoors. It doesn't matter where you are. You are lying on your back and looking up at the sun in the sky. Just focus on the sun – look at the huge yellow dot in the sky.

I want you to know that your special mind can do anything you want it to do. You can change anything if you really want to. Tell me what your favourite colour is.

(Guidance note: if the child says yellow, ask them what is their second favourite colour)

So look at the yellow dot in the sky again. Change it from yellow to your favourite colour. See what your special mind has done – it has changed the colour. So it can change other things too if you would like it to.

(Guidance note: I shall use blue for the rest of the script)

Keep looking at that lovely blue dot in the sky. Look deep into it and feel how relaxing it is to look at that colour. That blue dot is full of relaxation and calmness, and that dot is going to send a warm blue glow of relaxation down from the sky to relax both your special mind and your body.

Keep looking at the blue dot; feel that glow of blue coming down and reaching the top of your head. Imagine the glow going through every strand of hair on the top of your head and moving gently through the skin and then into the inside of your head and reaching into your special mind. Feel the blue glow relaxing your mind as it moves round and round into every part of your mind, which is becoming more and more relaxed. Letting go of any thoughts – just relaxing – not a care in the world.

As your mind is relaxing more and more the blue glow is going to continue working its way down your body – inside and out – to relax every part of you.

Moving gently and slowly – down and down. Over your forehead. Over your eyes as your eyelids are getting heavier and heavier in a very pleasant way. At the same time the blue glow is travelling down both sides of your head – over each ear and going directly into your ears and into your ear canals.

Now it's moving down over your cheeks and over your mouth. Relaxing your teeth and your jaw. Some people clench or grind their teeth when they are worried or stressed. Just let your jaw drop a little. Just relax more and more as the blue glow continues to move gently and slowly.

Feel the blueness going down the back of your head, deep into your neck – the knotty bit at the top of your spine. Stretching outwards into your shoulders, collar bone and shoulder blades. Give your shoulders a shake if you want to. Just relax them – don't scrunch them up. Relax.

The blue glow is continuing to travel down and down the outside of your body, but at the same time it is going into the pores of your skin and getting inside your body. Getting into your bones – deep into the marrow at the centre of each bone. Into all your muscles – so they become so floppy – so very very floppy.

After going through your skin, the blue glow gets into your veins and blood. The blood carries the relaxation and goodness from the blue glow round and round your body. The blue glow is being pumped through your healthy heart.

Now feel the blue glow moving to the top of your arms and then travelling down each arm – slowly and gently. Relaxing every muscle – becoming floppier and floppier. Trying to reach your elbows. Now moving down and down towards the lower part of your arms; stretching towards your wrists. Stretching towards your hands – trying to reach your fingertips – and when the blue glow gets there you might experience a very pleasant tingling sensation.

Realise now that the blue glow is moving down both the front and back of your body. Feel the relaxation moving over your chest and stomach, but remember the blueness is moving on the inside too. Imagine the relaxation going into all your vital organs – heart, kidneys, liver and lungs. Also your stomach, bowel and intestine; all the parts of you that are working so well and in harmony. Feel all the muscles in your stomach go floppy – really floppy.

Bring your attention to your back now. Your spine is a very complicated thing – it has bones, tiny vertebrae and even little gaps in between. All held together by muscles. Imagine the blue glow penetrating the bones – getting right down into the marrow – feel all the bones truly relaxing. The blue glow gets into each little vertebra. The relaxation and goodness are getting into all those tiny gaps. The muscles holding your spine upright go all floppy – relaxing completely.

Now the blue glow continues to work its way down the rest of your body. Moving slowly and gently – relaxing you more and more. Travelling down and down towards your legs. Relaxing your thigh muscles back and front. Down and down towards your knees and knee caps – getting deep into the bones there.

Down and down further into the lower part of your legs. Into your calf muscles – just feel the blue glow relaxing them. People often clench their calf muscles when they are tense – just feel those muscles go all floppy now. At the same time your shin bones on both legs relax. The blue glow is going deep into the bones and muscles. Stretching slowly and gently towards your ankles.

Now the blue glow is stretching towards your feet. Still moving slowly and gently. Stretching more and more trying to reach your toes, and as it does you might experience that pleasant tingling session both in your toes and your fingers again.

Now that your whole body is completely relaxed from head to toe, imagine that you are looking down at your feet. Whatever you imagine is on your feet – trainers, shoes, boots, socks – just place them to one side so you are left looking at your two bare feet.

Look at your right foot.

(Guidance note: for smaller children just ask them to choose one foot)

Look at the skin on the top of it. Look at the skin covering your foot. You may think it is all one colour but it isn't. There are different shades of dark and light in the skin. Look for patterns and shapes. Now look at the outside of your right foot; take a journey around the outside of your foot – be aware of the different shapes and bumps. Now focus on your toes – each individual toe. Look at the size and shape of each one – the five of them are all different. Look at each toe nail – the shape, the colour – look for patterns within each toe nail.

Now look at your left foot (*or other foot*). Look at the skin on the top of it. Look at the skin covering your foot. You may think it is all one colour but it isn't. There are different shades of dark and light in the skin. Look for patterns and shapes. Now look at the outside of your left/other foot; take a journey around the outside of your foot – be aware of the different shapes. Now focus on your toes – each individual toe. Look at the size and shape of each one – the five of them are all different. Look at each toe nail – the shape, the colour – look for patterns within each toe nail.

Wiggle your toes on both feet. They are perfectly relaxed but they are also ready to take you anywhere you want to go. So your whole body is now perfectly relaxed and calm – ready to go wherever you want to go now…

Chapter 5

Exploring the island in the city

Introduction

This script can be used for general relaxation purposes but is also useful for assessment as the hypnotherapist can gain an insight into the modalities i.e. as to the whether the child is visual, auditory, kinaesthetic, olfactory and gustatory. It can be used purely as a guided script but in the text I have inserted some questions, so the hypnotherapist can talk in more depth with the child as they explore the island and gain more insight into the modalities.

The script

I just want you to sit back and close your eyes when you feel ready. It can be good to be busy doing things but sometimes it is nice to slow down too; to relax and use your imagination. To help you relax today we are going to explore a city – take a nice gentle walk.

I wonder what a city looks like to you. Just let your wonderful imagination think of a city. What do think of first? People, animals or things? Buildings, houses, shops, churches, parks, cars, bicycles. Or do you think of something else?

Whilst you are thinking about a city I wonder if you can hear any noises. Or can you smell anything?

I know a big city which has lots of interesting things in it. This city has a river running right through the middle of it; there are lots of steep hills, which makes it extremely difficult to walk up the roads – people get very puffed and out of breath. Some cars that don't have big engines stutter and stop when trying to drive up the steep roads.

In the very centre of the city there are lots of buildings – both old and new. I wonder if you can imagine some of these buildings. Perhaps you would like to imagine walking up to take a closer look at some of the buildings. I wonder what you are seeing. Shops. Cafes. Restaurants. Hotels. Banks. This particular city has two cathedrals – one of them has a very tall pointed steeple; the other one has a big tower with lots of bells in it.

The city is always busy – it never sleeps. It is full of life and very exciting things. There are lots of interesting things to see and things to do. I wonder what you would like to do in this city you are imagining now.

28　Exploring the island in the city

Now this big city has lots of different parts to it and there is one very special part known as the island. Perhaps you would like to go there now. Just imagine that you are moving away from the busy city centre. It does not matter how you move to get there – you can do anything in your imagination – so you choose how you are going to move – walk, fly – anyway you like.

However you are moving you are going to go past one of the cathedrals. This cathedral has a very big tower, with lots of bells inside it. Can you hear the bells ringing? If you look up maybe you can see some birds sitting on top of the tower. Are they singing? Can you look even higher into the sky? What colour is the sky? Are there any clouds? Do you see anything else high up in the sky?

Now you are going to go down a very steep pathway which runs alongside this cathedral. As you go down the side of the cathedral you take some nice deep breaths. Slowly breathe in *1, 2* and *3* and then gently breathe out *3, 2,* and *1*. Just relaxing with each outbreath as you go. Going down and down the steep pathway.

At the bottom you come to a road. If you look across the road you can see the river. The river is flowing gently and slowly – just watch it for a moment. It is so relaxing watching the river. Watch the steady flow – making you feel more and more relaxed. Now just keep moving towards the river – watch out for any cars or bicycles that might be on the road. As you get nearer to the river you see a big sign which says: 'This way to the island in the city'.

You are feeling nice and relaxed now; with each movement forward that you take you are just letting go of any cares or worries you may have. You may also be feeling a little bit excited about going to find the island. It is always good to find new places to explore in your imagination. So just keep following the signs you see to the island and as you go look to the right and to the left – what do you see?

As you move on a little further you know instinctively that when the road bends you will be on the island.

There are lots of things to see and do on the island. I am sure you are going to find things that I don't know about. There is always something to see, find and do. Just keep moving...

(Guidance note: here the hypnotherapist can choose to divert to another script to work on a particular issue or carry on for general deepening)

Now I am going to tell you about some of the places I know on the island. The river flows around and right through the middle of it too. You might be able to see some of the animals that live and work in the water or on the riverbank.

The river divides the island and to get from one side to the other you have to cross the beautiful old bridge. On special days the bridge gets closed for a street market. Cars and bicycles cannot cross the bridge on those days but people come from all over to buy from the stalls. Look at those stalls on the bridge now. What are they selling?

Human beings live on both sides of the island too. There are all sorts of houses, apartments and studios – different shapes and sizes.

On one side of the island there is a lot of work going on in the business centre, the factories, and the garage where they repair damaged cars. Some people come to the island to keep fit because there is a place where people can climb up a very high wall. Next to the climbing wall building you may be able to see the pet shop that has lots of interesting fish in the tanks which line the walls. Can you see any other pets in there?

On the other side of the river there is a huge very old museum. It has lots of interesting things to see and touch, so you can learn all about the past and how local people made things.

You can also learn a lot, see beautiful things and play with paints and crafts by visiting the art gallery.

Then there is a brewery where they make beer and put it in barrels, big bottles and small bottles. You can always smell the beer being brewed when you pass by. Can you smell it now? Some people like the smell; others think it is horrible. Lots of people visit the island just to buy or drink the tasty beer.

On both sides of the island there are also lots of places to eat and drink – can you see them? Can you smell any food or drink as you are walking by the coffee shops, cafes and restaurants? Is this making you feel hungry or thirsty? Can you taste anything in your mouth? Would you like to go inside somewhere for something to eat or drink?

So you have experienced a lot on the island on your first visit and as you have been moving around and exploring you have become more and more relaxed. You can come back here anytime for another visit – when you want to slow down a bit, relax. You can go back to some of the places you have already seen today or you may want to look for other places. You can start in the city centre like you did today, move down by the cathedral and go towards the river. Just let your imagination take you anywhere you want to go…

Chapter 6

The flea market

Introduction

A properly trained hypnotherapist knows that it is imperative to build rapport with a client and undertake a thorough assessment before deciding the best way to work with him or her. With children it is so important to have some knowledge about their interests before you even meet them and then build on that during the assessment. I said in the introduction to this book one of my main aims is to get children to use their imaginations more, rather than relying on electronic devices to entertain themselves. Before that can happen in the therapy room the hypnotherapist has to get them interested and talking. Depending on the child's age I will do this by engaging in play (and have a wide range of toys available in the therapy room) and drawing.

Once I have undertaken the assessment and want to introduce the child to trance I have found using objects is a great way to get a child focussed. Objects I commonly use are:

- Wands (glitter wands used for autism/ADHD are useful aids to get any child focussed on colours, stars, bubbles and movement)
- Feathers
- Squares of felt
- Leaves
- Flowers/petals
- Pieces of wood/bark from a tree/twigs.

It is not always necessary to use actual objects; the purpose of this script is to encourage the child to use an object they find in their imagination whilst walking around the flea market.

The script

I want you to imagine that you are taking a walk and your mission is to find an unusual and interesting object. You could look for something as you walk along but I know a really good place that has all sorts of interesting things to look at – it's called the flea market. You need to look out for a huge building that has a very wide entrance – during the daytime the door is never closed.

Imagine you are standing on the pavement outside this huge building and look inside. How amazingly full of stuff this place is. Things are piled up high – all sorts of things – chairs; tables; lights; lampshades; light fittings; bookcases; fridges; and cookers. So many things.

In between all these things there are smaller objects too – old vinyl records; videos; CDs; DVDs; books; pieces of jewellery; old clothes; shoes; curtains; vases; statues, plates and cups. Some things are in boxes others are just sitting on the floor.

So go on your mission now. Walk around the flea market and find one interesting and unusual object. Take your time and then tell me when you have found something and what it is.

Now find a nice comfy chair to sit in; there are plenty to choose from in the flea market. Take (*the object*) with you. Hold (*the object*) very still in both your hands and look down at it. Take some nice deep breaths – in and out. Breathing slowly and deeply helps you to concentrate more on (*the object*). Shut out any sounds around you. Just look at (*the object*) – still holding it very still in both your hands.

Look at the shape of (*the object*). Follow the outline of (*the object*). Imagine what the edge(s) of it feels like.

Look at the colour(s) you can see.

The more you concentrate on looking at the object the harder it is to keep your eyes open. Your eyelids are beginning to feel very heavy.

Is anything moving?

(*Guidance note: only use this question if the object has something inside it e.g. if you are using a glitter wand*)

When you feel you can't keep your eyelids open any longer just let your object drop into your lap.

Chapter 7

Relaxing on the riverbank
Having some quiet time

Introduction

The main objective in using this script is to help a child relax. Younger children in particular can have boundless energy and then suddenly they may just fall asleep. However, some children have particular problems which make it difficult for them to relax or get to sleep. So this is a really good script to use with a child who presents as being hyperactive and for those who have been diagnosed with a particular issue e.g. said to be on the autistic spectrum; having attention deficit hyperactivity disorder (ADHD) or Asperger's Syndrome.

Nowadays, children of all ages can find it hard to wind down because they are constantly being stimulated by technology and they become dependent on it (sometimes addicted to it) for entertainment. A lot of children tell me they are on their phones or iPads until they decide to go to sleep and then they cannot get to sleep. This is because whatever they have been doing or watching has stimulated them rather than relaxed them. This script will help a child to use their imagination (rather than technology) to rest or go to sleep.

I think it is imperative that the hypnotherapist factors in enough time in a session to have some in-depth discussions in the conscious state. Suggestions will be made in the hypnotic state, but I find it useful to have discussions with a child about how and when they use their devices and how it can be beneficial to take some time out just to relax by going into trance. A child needs to learn the benefits of true relaxation and this can be achieved by the hypnotherapist encouraging them to go into trance regularly during the day so it becomes part of their lifestyle. This is especially helpful to those children who are revising and preparing for exams. They should not feel guilty about taking some time out for themselves.

It is also important to help the child understand that they need to prepare for sleep i.e. gradually wind down, rather than just expecting it to happen automatically after they have finished whatever they have been doing.

It is the job of the hypnotherapist to help the child discover that using trance is a great way to relax and that going into trance on a regular basis can become part of one's life to promote a better sense of wellbeing. I always make sure that there is enough time both at the beginning and at the end of a session to have discussions in the conscious state. Hypnotherapists need to be mindful to allocate enough time for their sessions and perhaps leave a longer period of time between booked appointments so no-one (the child or hypnotherapist) feels rushed or that time is running out.

The script

It is fantastic that you have so much energy and like to play a lot, but sometimes it is just nice to sit back and relax a bit. It is very good for you to let your mind just drift and have some *quiet time*. Drift off to anywhere you want to go – and imagine. I know for sure that you have a terrific imagination that can take you anywhere – on an exciting adventure, to a favourite place or maybe to have a conversation with somebody. But today I want you to just relax and let your special mind drift, because your special mind is like the rest of your body – each part needs to rest in order to make it strong and healthy for the future. Your mind needs *quiet time*.

I want you to imagine a river; and on one side of the river there is a riverbank. It is just so nice to sit on a riverbank and look around. I wonder if you would like to imagine you are on the riverbank now. So while you are doing that, I want to tell you about Desi the duck, and her twelve ducklings.

Now Desi's ducklings had loads of energy just like you and it was hard for Desi to keep her eye on all twelve of them all of the time. She loved that they had lots of energy, always waddling off to look at things, digging deep with their little beaks, sometimes getting into mischief as all ducklings do; but Desi was firm that the ducklings (as well as herself) needed *quiet time*.

So when it was time for *quiet time* Desi would get the ducklings lined up. They always waddled in pairs behind her. She would take them for a walk along the riverbank to a space which was hidden away in between two very large trees, but had a great view of the river.

Desi then got the ducklings to spread out from each other and asked them to sit down on the lovely luscious grass which was in this space. There were always one or two of the ducklings who did not want to do this because they would rather be playing than have *quiet time*, but they were all good little ducklings so they did whatever their mother asked them to do. Once they sat down on the lovely luscious grass Desi then spoke to them in her *gentle, soothing, relaxing* voice:

> Just look at the river in front of you. Don't look around just watch the water. The water which is bobbing up and down – flowing in front of you. Look at the different shapes you can see on the surface of the water. Pick a shape and watch it flow until it is out of sight. Now find another one and follow it until it is out of sight – and another one – and as you are doing this your eyelids are becoming heavier and heavier. Keep finding the shapes and when you cannot keep your eyes open any longer just let them close, relax your feathers – every single one of them – and relax your beak by just letting it open a little bit.

Just imagine Desi talking to the ducklings in her *gentle, soothing, relaxing* voice and see the ducklings one by one closing their eyes and relaxing; some of them moving on to their sides and stretching out – totally relaxed.

Imagine now you are on the riverbank with Desi and her ducklings. Just get yourself settled on the lovely luscious grass – that's right. Now listen to Desi's *gentle, soothing, relaxing* voice:

> Just look at the river in front of you. Don't look around just watch the water. The water which is bobbing up and down – flowing in front of you. Look at the different shapes you can see on the surface of the water. Pick a shape and watch it flow until it is out of sight. Now find another one and follow it until it is out of sight – and another one – and as you are doing this your eyelids are becoming heavier and heavier. Keep finding the shapes and when you cannot keep your eyes open any longer just let them close. Now relax every part of your body – just let everything go really floppy. Start with your legs – your toes and feet. Your arms – your fingers and thumbs. Your tummy. Your back. Your head and shoulders. Just as floppy as they can be.

Now that your body is *relaxing* so well you can let that mind of yours relax too. Just let it drift – not worrying about anything at all – not really thinking about anything at all – just *relaxing* and having *quiet time*.

Chapter 8

Fire

Introduction

I have included four scripts which focus on using a fire to attain the therapeutic objectives the hypnotherapist is trying to achieve with the child. A fire can give a sense of warmth and comfort, but it can also be a very powerful tool to use in the imagination. However, some children may have had a bad experience with a flame, fire or firework i.e. they have been burnt themselves or seen someone else have an accident. In these circumstances it would not be appropriate to use any of these scripts.

The first two scripts offer ways of getting a child into trance by focussing on the fire and then deepening. Script 1 is a simple and quick way of achieving this using a fire and fireplace indoors. Script 2 is for a child who likes the outdoors and to be active.

It is a sad fact that some very young children have never actually seen a traditional open fire because they are being brought up in homes which have central heating. Some children may not understand what coal or a coal fire is, so the hypnotherapist needs to do some checking out before using Script 1. This script is a gentle way of getting the child into trance by focusing on a coal fire within a fireplace. If the hypnotherapist knows that the child has a log burner in their house then the script can be adapted i.e. replacing the coal fire with the log burner.

Both Scripts 1 and 2 can be followed by one of the additional scripts in order to do more in-depth work. The first additional script uses the fire already created in the imagination to get rid of something by burning it in the fire e.g. thought, feeling, behaviour or a particular memory. This script is particularly helpful for children who have been abused. The second additional script can facilitate taking the child on a journey to undertake some regression work or for forward pacing. Again, this script works well to help the healing process of a child who has experienced abuse and to promote their wellbeing for the future.

Script 1: Fire in the living room

I want you to imagine that it is the middle of winter. It is very cold outside and it is just starting to snow. You have no need to worry about the cold or the snow because you are imagining that you are in a living room, which is cosy and warm. Somewhere in this living room there is very large fireplace and a lit, burning coal fire to keep you cosy and warm. Have a look around the living room and then find a comfortable chair you would like to sit in – maybe you might like to find some cushions too. Now place the chair right in front of the fireplace, but not too close. Gently take a deep breath in and sink into the lovely comfortable chair. Then breathe out gently and you sink further down – so relaxing.

While you are starting to relax even more – feeling cosy and warm – just look at the fireplace. See whether it is old or modern; what colour it is; what it is made of. Does it have anything placed on the top of it? Is there anything at the bottom of it?

Now look into the burning fire. Look deep into the burning fire. See the coals burning. Look even deeper into the fire. See the dancing flames and the beautiful rich colours within them – yellow; orange; red; blue and purple. Look to the edges of the fire where some of coals have not started burning yet. Look at the deep silky blackness of the coals. What else can you see in the fire?

Now feel the warmth coming out of the fire – reaching your face and hands – so soothing. The more you look into the fire and watch the flames you feel all your bones and muscles in your body relaxing. Every part of you is relaxing and becoming floppy. Feel the floppiness in your head – your arms – your legs – the top half of your body – then the lower half of your body. Really really floppy. Your hands are floppy. Your feet are floppy. Now your whole body is floppy and relaxed.

As you keep on looking deeper and deeper into the fire you are feeling cosy and warm – feeling more and more relaxed, calm and safe. Feeling cosy – warm – relaxed – calm and safe.

Script 2: Camp fire

I know you like to be outside doing lots of different activities, so I want you to imagine that you are on a camping trip. You have travelled to a beautiful forest and you have already set up camp. Look at the outside of your tent – securely fixed with pegs. Now look inside the tent and make sure you have everything you need – sleeping bag; pillow; bottle of water; a torch.

Come back out of the tent. You will see your rucksack – full of things you might need – change of clothes; wash things; toothbrush; toothpaste; first aid kit. Near your rucksack, already laid out on the ground are food items and bottles of water; other drinks; cutlery; plates and cups. There is also a camping table and a camping chair for you to use.

Now it is time to make a fire. So you need to go and find some wood, sticks, twigs, dry leaves, and anything else you might find that will make a good fire. Tell me what you find as you explore the forest and what you are going to use.

Good – well done.

Now start to build the fire. Tell me how you are doing it as you go along.

Right – is the fire ready to be lit? You need to find some matches. I wonder where they will be – maybe in your rucksack.

Before you light the fire, place the camping chair somewhere where you will get a good look at the fire once it starts to burn. OK – so light the fire now and then go to sit down in the camping chair.

See where the flames start to burn – slowly at first, but then they rise up and they start to spread. See the (*whatever the child has put on the fire e.g. wood, sticks, twigs, leaves*) start to catch fire. The flames are spreading – the flames are strong and bright;

gaining strength as they spread upwards and outwards. As the flames become more powerful you feel the warmth they give off. Feel the warmth coming towards your face – your hands – your feet. The flames are gaining in strength and energy; as they do so they move more quickly – more powerfully.

Watch the flames rise up and up. Look deep into the fire. See all the different colours within the fire. The unburnt (*e.g. wood, sticks, twigs, leaves*) – grey, brown, black and green. The rising flames – yellow; orange; red; blue and purple. The spiralling smoke – grey, white and black. Feel the warmth again reaching your face – your hands – your feet.

I wonder if you can smell anything as the fire continues to burn – growing in strength and energy – becoming more powerful.

Watching the fire burn is so fascinating, but also so relaxing. Keep watching as long as you want. Just relax more and more, become calmer and calmer. At the same time, you also feel strength and energy spreading deep within you – just likes the flames of fire – becoming more and more powerful.

(Guidance note: the hypnotherapist can choose to embed commands at this point or use one of the additional scripts below to undertake more specific work)

Additional script 1: Burning stuff

A fire is a good place to get rid of things. So think about what you would like to get rid of (*or insert issue already discussed*).

(Guidance note: for younger children it will be enough to throw whatever it is onto the fire. For older children more in-depth work can be undertaken using the following questions:

What is the reason you want to get rid of this?
What has it done to you in the past?
How did that make you feel?
How will getting rid of this help you?
What do you want for the future?
How are you going to achieve this?)

Imagine that (X *i.e. whatever the child is going to get rid of*) is in front of you. Put (X) in the fire and see it burn. As you watch it burn you feel a sense of ease – letting go of something that has held you back. You feel tranquil and at peace as you see (X) disappear completely into the flames of the fire. Watch closely as the flames consume (X). See (X) burn and disappear completely. It feels so good to let go of things. Tell me when (X) has disappeared completely.

How do you feel now that X has gone?

(Guidance note: the hypnotherapist can then embed some positive commands)

Additional script 2: Fireworks and the rocket

So, it is night-time and as you are relaxing so comfortably beside the camp fire you look up to the dark sky and for some unknown reason you start thinking about fireworks – and how pretty they can make the dark sky.

So why don't you make your own firework display? Your imagination can create anything you want. Imagine some rockets lifting off from the ground and soaring high into the sky. Look up into the sky and tell me what happens. What do you see?

What colours are there?
Do you see any different shapes – stars perhaps?
Are the fireworks noisy?
Do you hear some bangs?

Something distracts you and takes your attention away from the sky. You see something spinning on the trunk of a tree nearby. Going round and round – very very fast. Giving off sparks and lots of different pretty colours. It's a Catherine wheel spinning round and round very fast.

Now somewhere in the pile of fireworks which are going to be in this firework display there is a very special rocket that has been made just for you. Just go over to the pile of fireworks and see if you can find it – it will have your name on it. Tell me when you have found it.

Now special powder has been put in this rocket so that it can travel anywhere you want to go. All you have to do is say the word 'Go' and then tell the rocket where you want to go. The rocket can go very fast indeed, so you can get you to places quickly if you need to do so and get yourself away from anything that you do not want think about.

Or maybe you might like to just let the rocket take you on a magical, mystery journey.

Would you like to have a ride on the rocket now?
Where would you like to go?

Off you go on your journey. Test the rocket out. See how fast it can go.
(Guidance note: the hypnotherapist at this point can then use the rocket to take the child on a specific journey i.e. either forwards in time or backwards for regression work)

Chapter 9

The maze

Introduction

The beginning of this script can be used simply as an induction and deepener or more in-depth work can be undertaken using the maze to address problems in relation to feeling:

- Confused
- Unable to make a decision
- Hopeless
- Trapped/no way out
- No point to anything.

This script embeds the idea that it is alright to take time to make a decision; no-one should be forced or rushed to make a decision when they are unsure about something. It is a script of optimism, that is, there is always a solution and a way out; it just might take some time to achieve this.

The hypnotherapist can use the maze in more than one session with a child, whilst they are undertaking ongoing work, trying to make a decision or deciding which pathway to take.

The script

Sometimes things can get a bit confusing and you can feel a bit lost – maybe you feel like you do not know which way to go. It's important to just take your time and let things happen naturally – when the time is right you will know which direction to take. In the meantime, it helps to relax and not to worry about the future and making decisions. Just let things happen naturally. So I think you might like to take a walk in a place where you can have some fun and it does not matter which direction you go or how long it takes you to find the way out.

I want you to imagine that you are in the grounds of a very big house, which has been owned by dukes and lords for hundreds of years. Maybe you can see the big house in the distance. There is a long straight gravel path leading up to the house which is on a slight hill. Just start walking along the path and you will notice that there are several little gravel pathways which run off to both sides of the main path. As you walk along, I want you to look out for a place which has lots of very high green hedges.

40 The maze

You will notice that the hedges form a pattern and between the hedges are pathways to walk along. Tell me when you see this place.

Good – you have found the maze. This is very exciting – you can have lots of fun exploring the maze. The maze has lots of different pathways going in many directions. Some pathways come to a dead end so you have to turn back and find another way. You might find that some of the hedges have holes or archways in them so you can take a short cut through and find a different path. The maze can be quite confusing at times but there is always a way out.

Walk down the gravel pathway which takes you to the maze and then find the entrance. Take your time there is no rush. Just tell me when you find the entrance.

Now when you are ready I want you take a really deep breath – enter the maze – and start walking forward.

Look how high the hedges are and as you are doing that notice the beautiful green leaves – all the different shapes and sizes. Sometimes you can find some holly and berries (like you see at Christmas time) within the hedges – have a good look and see if you can see any.

As you keep walking along I wonder what else you might see – the soil underneath the hedges; some flowers that have grown in the soil. The hedges of the maze make you feel safe and secure. You know that there may be many pathways in the maze but there is always a way out. Look right up – high above your head and see the beautiful clear blue sky; the sun is shining brightly. You feel the sun's warmth on your skin.

I wonder what else you might you see as you continue to walk. Look around you – above you – in front of you – and on the floor. I wonder if you see any animals – birds, squirrels, a hedgehog perhaps, or even a wriggly worm in the soil.

Can you hear any noises? Other people chattering. Bees buzzing. Birds singing or flapping their wings. A slight breeze perhaps. An aeroplane high up in the sky.

Now the maze is fun because you can enjoy just walking as you have been doing and noticing all the lovely things around you. But another reason it is fun is – at some point you have got to find your way out. This is not always a simple task but it will be fun to do because as you walk around the maze you will have to keep making decisions about which direction to take. Sometimes you will just know which way to go – it will feel right. At other times you may feel puzzled or confused because you feel you have been down this pathway before. Some of the pathways and hedges may look the same.

Remember there is always a way out. All you have to do is take your time, keep calm and relaxed and think about things. There is no need to rush at all. You will know what to do. Just take your time because it is good not to rush into something. Just remain calm and relaxed whilst you think about which direction to take.

You might find yourself coming to some dead ends – where there is a hedge blocking the pathway. You will have to turn back and find another pathway to take you in another direction. Remember there will be unexpected helpful short cuts within the hedges – holes and archways – you just have to find them. Take your time – there is no need to rush at all.

So which way are you going to go first?

(Guidance note: at this point the hypnotherapist has the option to continue to use the maze as a deepener OR to undertake more in-depth work regarding experience and feelings on his/her journey through the maze. It is important to ask certain questions

about the child's feelings as they work their way around the maze and utilise any experiences discussed previously. Some of the following questions/prompts may prove to be helpful)

Just throw away that feeling of ... (e.g. feeling lost; no sense of direction; frustration; hopelessness).
You have reached a dead end. What will you do now? Which way will you go?
How do you feel?
What do you want to do?
You can bring in things to help you. What or who might they be?
You know there is always a way out. Not just one way – several ways.
Take your time – there is no need to rush.
Think about what you are looking for.
What do you know already?
What have you learnt from before (insert previous experience)?
Find a shortcut if you want to or if you think that would be helpful to you.
Now suddenly you can see the way out. How do you feel about that?

Additional script 1: Deepening in the maze

Look along this pathway you are on. Focus on the far end and you can see that a part of the hedge is missing. It is like someone has cut a huge piece out of it and now there are two separate hedges. Walk towards this big gap and stop when you get there. Look down and you will see there are steps going down – this is just one way out of the maze, but this particular way is going to take you into another place where you are going to feel even more calm and relaxed.

There are ten steps down and there is a rail to use if you want to do so. The steps are well made and strong – you are completely safe.

10: Take the first step
 9: Going down – feeling relaxed – feeling safe
 8: Taking another step now – feeling even more relaxed
 7: Relaxing more and more
 6: Going down further – feeling really relaxed
 5: Halfway there now – going deeper and deeper
 4: Down and down
 3: More and more relaxed
 2: Feeling very very safe
 1: When I say zero you will step off the last step
 0.

Chapter 10

The beards

Introduction

This is just a fun script to be used as a deepener. It is really important to check that the child does not have a problem with or phobia about beards.

The script

There were a father and son who had very unusual beards. They spent a lot of time together because they lived in the same house and at the back of the house there was a workshop where they made and sold cutlery – knives, forks and spoons. People liked to come to look at the cutlery but they were always more fascinated by the men's beards.

I wonder if you can imagine what the men and their beards looked like. Imagine that you are holding a photograph in your hand and see the two men's faces in front of you.

Now look at the older man first. Look at the shape of his face. His eyes – what colour are they? His nose – is it long or short? Is it straight or crooked? His mouth – is it open or closed? Does he have thin or thick lips?

I want you to focus on the older man's beard. Have a good look at it. What colour is it? Are there different shades of (*colour*) in the beard? Does the older man keep his beard short and neat or bushy and long? Can you tell me – is his beard shiny or dull?

Now you are going to focus on the shape of the beard. So choose one side of the older man's face to look at the beard there. How many hairs can you see – perhaps you could start counting them (*pause*). Then follow the beard around – look at the different parts of the man's face it covers. I wonder if you can see shapes and patterns in the beard as you look at the man's cheeks, mouth, jaw and chin. Look how far down the beard goes. Does it stop at his chin or does it go under his chin and onto his neck; or does it just hang off his face a long way down?

Now look at the younger man. Look at the shape of his face. His eyes – what colour are they? His nose – is it long or short? Is it straight or crooked? His mouth – is it open or closed? Does he have thin or thick lips?

I want you to focus on the younger man's beard. Have a good look at it. What colour is it? Are there different shades of (*colour*) in the beard? Does the younger man keep his beard short and neat or bushy and long? Can you tell me – is his beard shiny or dull?

Now you are going to focus on the shape of the beard. So choose one side of the younger man's face to look at the beard there. How many hairs can you see – perhaps you could start counting them (*pause*). Then follow the beard around – look at the different parts of the man's face it covers. I wonder if you can see shapes and patterns in the beard as you look at the man's cheeks, mouth, jaw and chin. Look how far down the beard goes. Does it stop at his chin or does it go under his chin and onto his neck or does it just hang off his face a long way down?

A beard is a bit like a forest; it's a good place to take a pleasant, relaxing walk. So I wonder which beard you would like to take a walk in – the father or the son's beard? Just imagine that you have magical powers to make yourself very light – light as air, so you don't weigh anything at all. You are lighter than a feather. So now you can jump onto the (*father/son's*) beard and the man won't even know you are there. So do it – jump into the beard.

Now walk down into the beard – deeper and deeper. Make your way down the strands of hair – sliding gently and slowly. Just take your time. As you go further into the beard down and down, you are feeling warm, comfortable and relaxed. You are feeling warm, comfortable and relaxed.

I wonder if you can smell anything – maybe a sweet smell from wax or beard oil that the man might have used or any other smells. Food smells. Drink smells.

As you make your way through the beard I wonder if you can see any shapes or find any objects – maybe a breadcrumb or a bit of crisp. What do you find?

As you go deeper can you hear any sounds? Perhaps the man's breathing; noises in the man's throat as he swallows, yawns or coughs. Is he talking – what is he saying? Is he singing – what is he singing? Can you hear anything else?

Continue now to go deeper and deeper into the beard…

(Guidance note: the hypnotherapist can then continue with the session as the child is now relaxed)

Chapter 11

Traffic lights

Introduction

I first wrote another version of this script when working with a particular exam anxiety group. The members of the group were convinced they were going to fail their GSCEs and a commonality was that they all had repetitive negative thoughts. It was like they all had their own negative mantra:

- *I'm going to fail*
- *I can't do this*
- *I'm stupid*
- *I'm not good enough.*

Alongside these negative thoughts ran sleepless nights or disturbed sleep caused by the repetitive thinking. The script worked well with this particular group; then I used it regularly with other exam anxiety groups and it became part of the programme.

The script below is written to work with children on a one-to-one basis to stop not only intrusive thoughts but also any feelings and behaviours which are occurring on a regular basis. This script works well because it gives a child an immediate strategy to use, and the feedback I usually get is about how instantly or quickly it worked and 'stopped things'.

I wrote this version of the script to focus mainly on stopping intrusive thoughts. However, it can be used to stop unwanted, recurring feelings and it is also possible to focus solely on behavioural changes if the hypnotherapist wishes this to be the main objective of the work.

The script is also helpful in facilitating the child to look forward. The hypnotherapist can help the child to look at how things can be changed and what they want to happen in the future so the child can move forward in a very positive way. To do this the hypnotherapist needs to do more in-depth work whilst working with the amber light before proceeding to the green light.

The script

Now you have been telling me about how you keep thinking about (*insert issue e.g. a particular thought, feeling, behaviour or situation*) a great deal and you would like it to stop. Your special mind has ways of dealing with things and I would like to help you with this. So just sit back and relax.

I would like to imagine that you are walking along a busy road. There is a lot of traffic on this road – cars, lorries, buses, bicycles – and it gets very jammed up because this is one of the main roads through a big city.

Just keep walking along – looking around you and listening to all the different noises. You then see that the traffic has stopped moving completely – it is not moving an inch. As you walk further on you see that there are traffic lights ahead of you. I am not sure what sort of traffic lights you will see because traffic lights can be built into the ground; or they can be overhead high up in the air; some stick out from a wall and then there are those temporary ones at roadworks that just sit on the road. Whatever type of traffic lights they are – they are your special traffic lights which are going to help you with (*the issue*).

I want you to go up to your set of traffic lights and stand so you can get a good view of the three coloured lights – red, amber and green. I want you to check out that the three lights are in good working order.

So look for the red light – see how bright it is. Then watch for the amber light to come on whilst the red light is still shining brightly. Nod when you see it come on. Now wait for the green light – and as it comes on the red and amber lights go out. Now look deeply into that green light. Good – so the lights are in good working order – working very efficiently. Just like your special mind.

Forget all about the traffic that is surrounding you – just let it drift off into the distance. Focus again on the traffic lights that are in front of you and just keep breathing nice and slowly – that's right – good. Now I want you to think about (*the issue*) which has been bothering you – just let those thoughts drift back in. Remember (*insert issue*) you were telling me about. Just stay with those thoughts and feelings for a short while.

Now a really good way to get rid of (*the issue*) is to look at the red traffic light. As soon as you see/feel/want to, (*the issue*) will *stop*. So let's try that. Think of (*the issue or use an actual situation if the child has talked about one*) – now see the red traffic light – look deep into the redness. Look for the different shades of dark and light in the red colour. I wonder if you can see any patterns.

Now I want you to make the amber light come on. Think about how you would like to feel (*insert from discussions with child*) and what you would like to do (*insert from discussions with child*). You can achieve anything you really want to do.

Think about what you want to change exactly. How are you going to do this?

(*Guidance note: the hypnotherapist can do some in-depth work with the child to work on the necessary changes and to project for the future. The amber light can be used to forward pace*)

Start to get *ready* and prepare to make those changes. Are you ready to do this? Are there any final changes or preparations you need to make?

When you are ready see the lights change to green and *go*. How good is that feeling (*reinforce with child's own words*)? Look at what you are doing. Feel those good feelings (*insert emotions/feelings*). You can feel like this any time you see the green light.

You can use the traffic lights at any time to get rid of any thoughts or feelings you don't like and make the changes you want. Just think 'Traffic Lights' and remember *stop – ready – go*.

Chapter 12

The workshop

Introduction

A hypnotherapy session is something a child should look forward to, not something they feel is a chore or something they *have* to do because their parents want them to attend. In reality this should not happen if the hypnotherapist has done sufficient preparation work in talking with the parents before an appointment is booked and then does a thorough assessment when meeting with the child for the first time.

Depending on the age of the child and if appropriate, I find it useful to have a brief chat on the phone with the child – not just the parents. Hypnotherapy will only work if the child wants to participate and work on something. It can be the case that a parent sees something (e.g. a behaviour like sucking a thumb) as a problem, but the child does not see it in the same way.

A hypnotherapy session should be fun but the child has to realise some work does need to be undertaken too. Also, some work has to be done in between sessions e.g. practising going into trance, going to a safe place, listening to a CD/track which has been made for them.

I have found it helpful when working with some children to create a workroom, which I call the workshop, so they know the work is being done here and then they can go off to other places in their imagination for fun before coming out of trance. This is particularly helpful for children who like to be organised and like routine, so they compartmentalise activities. The workshop is a safe place where difficult things can be talked about and worked on; and also where things can be left behind.

In my experience, children regularly imagine the workshop as something out of the ordinary e.g. a spaceship, a train, a dungeon or a laboratory. If the hypnotherapist is going to have several sessions with a child, then the workshop is a place where they can come back to each time and further work is undertaken. The hypnotherapist also needs to encourage the child to go there in between the sessions to work on the issues as agreed.

I have included a list of things which might be found and used in a workshop. The hypnotherapist can use things from this list as prompts to carry out certain therapeutic work or introduce props/items that might be of interest or help to the child. The child should also be encouraged to find equipment themselves.

The script

At times it can be good to separate out different things you need to do in your special mind. You will have your own way of thinking about things and your own way of doing things, but now and then you need to make some changes in order to make things better.

It is an absolute must that you have fun in your life and do things that make you happy and contented. But there are some things we have to do that maybe we don't want to do or things that we put off doing because we find them hard to do.

So in your special mind it can be good to imagine that you have a workshop – a place where you can work on things and get things done, then go somewhere else in your special mind to have some fun. So let's find your workshop.

Imagine that you are walking down a street – any street at all. As you walk along this street you see big streets and small streets running off to the left and the right, but there are also pathways and little alleyways that are easy to miss. So just explore and go in any direction you like. Enjoy relaxing as you explore and not really having to think about anything at all. Look around you and enjoy what you see, not worrying about anything at all. Just enjoy your walk.

As you walk along you know that eventually you will find your workshop – a place where you can work on things and get things done. Keep going – you will find your workshop. Keep going until you see a building – you know that your workshop will be in there. I have no idea what type of building it will be, but you will tell me when you see it. This is exciting, isn't it? Not knowing what sort of building you are going to find. Just keep walking until you come to it. Tell me when you see it.

Can you tell me what it looks like?

(Guidance note: use some prompts if required e.g. What is it made of? How many floors are there? How many doors? Are there any windows?)

How are you going to get into the building? When you are ready, in you go – 1, 2 and 3.

Start to look around because you need to find your workshop. Go and see what rooms you can find. Tell me what you find as you look around. Remember you are looking for your workshop – somewhere you can get things done.

How are you feeling as you are looking around this place and looking for your workshop?

Somewhere in this place there will be a room which is only used for working on things. Somewhere where you will want to work on things and achieve things. You might want to get rid of some stuff completely. You might want to make some changes. In your workshop you will be able to do all sorts of things. You will be able to make things happen. There will be all sorts of objects and equipment in your workshop to help you.

Tell me when you have found your workshop and when you are ready to go in.

1, 2 and 3 in you go.

What do you see?

(Guidance note: at this point it can be useful to introduce some of the following if required)

If you look around you might be able to find:

1. Desk
2. Chairs/sofa
3. Computer/laptop
4. iPad
5. Telephone

6. Television
7. Clock
8. Filing cabinets
9. A waste disposal unit
10. Levers
11. Buttons
12. Switches
13. Kitchen area
14. Books
15. All sorts of tools/equipment – whatever you need
16. Any other furniture.

(Guidance note: the hypnotherapist can now proceed to work on any issue using the equipment which has been found in the workshop and should encourage the child to look for other equipment/help – which can include people or animals)

Remember you can come back to your workshop at any time in the future to work on anything you want.

Chapter 13

A bit of stomping

Introduction

In my work I like to encourage a child to use their own language (which is going to be more meaningful and helpful to them) to develop mantras. I think this helps to embed commands further. With older children I do use the term 'mantra' which can be defined as:

- a word or sound repeated to aid concentration; a statement or slogan repeated frequently (Oxford English Dictionary)
- a word or phrase that is often repeated and expresses a particular strong belief (Cambridge English Dictionary)

The idea of introducing a mantra is so the child can reinforce belief in themselves and continue to work on their issue both in the conscious state as well as the hypnotic state.

Part of my work involves delivering training to professionals and workers from all sorts of backgrounds. A course I run regularly is Assertiveness Training and one of the exercises participants really like (although many find it strange at first) is the Stomping Exercise, which they do as a group. Some participants share the mantras they have developed in the morning session and later the group stomps out some of the mantras working in a circle – stomping round the room. By the end of it the whole group is energised.

For the purposes of assertiveness training mantras, I usually suggest that mantras should be no more than three to four words. In the circle, participants say the mantra out loud but walk in time to the words. The person whose mantra it is leads the circle and the rest of the group walk in pairs. They find a rhythm and then get quicker; they stomp rather than walk. The idea of stomping is to encourage motivation and determination. So this is the reason I thought this exercise could be translated into a script and it has worked well with many children of all ages. They seem to like having a stomp in their imagination but also in the real world.

I have set the script below in a school hall, but the hypnotherapist can suggest a different environment if a child does not like school or s/he has a particular interest. Younger children seem to like stomping around a circus ring; teenagers who enjoy exercising/sports often imagine a football pitch, a cricket ground, a running track in an athletic stadium or an ice-skating rink.

In the script I have used just one mantra as an example, a very common one: '*I am confident*'. Other mantras can be developed from:

I am…
I can…
I can be…
I shall…
I will…
I will be…
I want to…

The script

You have done a lot of good work today – well done. Now you know it is important to relax and listen to your CD/track in between our sessions, and think about things we have discussed. I'd like you to try out something now which is fun but it will also reinforce what you have done today.

You and your special mind have agreed/said (*insert phrase/mantra*).
(*Guidance note: for ease of reading the script I am going to use: 'I am confident'*)

Just imagine you are in the school hall. There is nobody else there. You have all the space to yourself. Go and stand at one end of the hall. Stand very still and say to yourself: '*I am confident*'. Keep standing still, feeling relaxed and say '*I am confident*' to yourself a few times. Good.

I want you to start walking around the hall in a big circle – quite slowly. As you start walking, I want you to say again: '*I am confident*'. That's exactly right. Now walk in time to what you saying. *I* (take one step) *-am* (take another step). The word 'confident' is a long word so you may need to take three steps for that: *con* (one step) *-fi* (another step) and *-dent* (third step). Try it out: *con* (one step) *-fi* (another step) and *-dent* (third step). *Con-fi-dent*.

Now put it all together and walk out: '*I* (step) *-am* (step) *con* (step) *-fi* (step) *-dent* (step)'. Great. Keep walking round in a big circle saying '*I am con-fi-dent*'. Hold your head up high and look straight ahead of you. Feel the confidence growing and expanding inside you with every step you take. That feels so good.

So go round the circle two more times – each time just getting a little bit faster, and pressing your feet down hard. Feeling the confidence rising up from your feet. Going right up both legs – through your toes, feet, shins and thighs. Now going into the trunk of your body. Going right up both your arms – through your fingers, hands, wrists, lower arms and upper arms. Now the confidence is reaching up through your neck and into your head. Keep putting your feet down really hard.

OK – I think you are now stomping. Stomping feels good. So now go even faster and you are saying out very loudly now: '*I am con-fi-dent*'. Still holding your head up high – looking straight ahead – feeling confident throughout your whole body. OK – just slow down gradually to a gentle walk again.

That was fun, wasn't it? Now you can have a stomp – a slow or quick one anytime you like; it is good to practise when you are doing the normal things at home, outside or at school, but you can imagine stomping in your imagination whenever you need to feel a boost of confidence. If you are on your own you can say '*I am con-fi-dent*' out loud, but if other people are around you can just say it silently in your head.

So now just imagine some of the places you will be during the next week and some of the activities you might be doing. Remember that stomping can be done silently. No-one needs to know you are stomping in your imagination. Can you tell me some of the places where you think you might have a bit of a stomp?
(Guidance note: if the child only comes up with one of or two places the hypnotherapist might want to make some other suggestions)

- Walking to school
- Places in school: classroom; gym; canteen
- At home: stairs; bedroom; garden
- Other places the child visits regularly/does activities (relatives'/friends' homes; clubs).

Well now you know a bit of stomping will help you feel confident whenever you need to in the future.

Chapter 14

The clock

Introduction

I have used this script for children who need time to go quicker; this can be for a variety of reasons. It may be that that they are worried or anxious about going for an appointment – perhaps at the dentist or at a hospital. Other children may be dreading a particular event; for example, attending a funeral, taking an exam or some form of test.

Using the clock can also work the other way i.e. to slow time down. When someone has exam anxiety and is worried that time is running out for revision or there is not enough time in an exam, it can be a distraction for them as they watch the hands of the clock. But using the clock can also demonstrate to the child how they can take control of things happening to them.

Therefore, the main objective in using this script is to help the child with the passing of time. However, it does not have to be used only to help with a problem. The clock can be used to help a child relive a good memory and for the future to slow things down in order to savour the experience and feelings associated with it.

The script

I just want you to imagine a clock – it can be anywhere you like – indoors or outdoors. I am wondering what the clock is like. Is it modern or is it very old? Is it big or is it small? What is it made of? What shape is it? What colour is it? Maybe there are different colours inside and outside the clock. Can you see the big hand and the little hand? What colour are the hands?

Just look around the outside of the clock – follow its shape – top to bottom and bottom to top. Slowly now – take your time – go round the outside of the clock. Looking at every little pattern or shape you can see. I wonder if the outside of the clock is rough or smooth. Can you feel it? Just nod when you have gone all the way around.

Now look deep into the clock's face – behind the big hand and the little hand. What colour is the clock's face? Look deep into the (*state colour child has said*) – see the different shades of dark and light in the clock face – behind the hands of the clock. That's right.

Now look at the big hand. Look at it from the very centre of the clock and follow it to the tip of the hand. What number is it pointing to?

Now look at the small hand. Look at it from the very centre of the clock and follow it to the tip of the hand. What number is it pointing to?

You know that your clever special mind can do anything it wants to do – it can *make* things happen. So make the big hand move round the clock. Watch the hand as it moves. Let it go round the clock just once. Tell me when it has stopped. Good. Now make the hand go round again but make it go very very fast. Gosh that was fast.

Now make the hand go round again but this time make it go very very slowly. As you are watching the big hand go round very very slowly, I want you to think about something. Time can seem to move differently. Sometimes it goes very fast; sometimes it goes very slow. Perhaps when you are really having fun and enjoying yourself (*insert some activities/interests you know the child has*) it all goes too quickly and ends too soon. Then when you are bored or fed up, time goes so slowly – it drags.

Well your clever special mind can help with this. You can experience time any way you want – fast or slow or whatever is just right for you. If you are really having fun you can make time slow down and enjoy every moment by making it last longer. And when you want something to be over very quickly you can make time go faster. You can make whatever you want to happen by looking at the clock and making the hands move faster or slower. First move the big hand – then move the little hand.

There is another way you can make the hands move too – by going inside the clock. Would you like to do that? Imagine that you have found a way into the back of the clock. You see all sorts of parts turning around – this way and that. Go and look at the different parts and find the part that makes the big hand of the clock work. Tell me when you have found it. Now look for the part that makes the little hand work. Tell me when you have found it. Now you can turn these parts to make the hands go faster or slower. Do you want to give it a try? Play and experiment with the parts and take control of time.

So you have two ways of controlling time now. You can look at the clock from the outside. Look straight at the clock face and tell the big hand and the little hand what to do. Or you can go inside the back of the clock and turn the parts to make the big hand and little hand move.

So let's just think about (*insert child's fear e.g. dental appointment; blood test; flight; exam*). Imagine yourself in that situation. Now see your clock and stand in front of it. Look at it carefully as you will have done many times before. Now focus on the big hand and with your clever special mind make it travel around the clock's face. Let it start slowly – and gradually – as it goes round the clock face make it go faster. That's right. Now make it go round again. It is going even faster this time and as it goes faster and faster you feel as though it is winding you down – feeling calmer and calmer; more relaxed in every way. The faster the clock's big hand goes, the more calm and more relaxed you feel as the time passes so very quickly.

You've made the big hand go very fast – do the same with the little hand. Let it start slowly – and gradually – as it goes round the clock face make it go faster. That's right. Now make it go round again. It is going even faster this time and as it goes faster and faster you feel as though it is winding you down – feeling calmer and calmer; more relaxed in every way. The faster the clock's little hand goes – the more calm and more relaxed you feel as the time passes so very quickly.

Would you like to try this from the inside of the clock now? You'll have a completely different view. You see the back of the clock face but you will still be able to see the hands moving. Take hold of the part that makes the big hand work and make the hand start moving slowly at first. Then make it go faster and faster. Now make it go round again. It is going even faster this time and as it goes faster and faster you feel as though it is winding you down – feeling calmer and calmer; more relaxed in every way. The faster the clock's big hand goes, the more calm and more relaxed you feel as the time passes so very quickly.

Staying in the back of the clock – take control of the part that makes the little hand work and make the hand start moving slowly at first. Then make it go faster and faster. Now make it go round again. It is going even faster this time and as it goes faster and faster you feel as though it is winding you down – feeling calmer and calmer; more relaxed in every way. The faster the clock's small hand goes, the more calm and more relaxed you feel as the time passes so very quickly.

You don't have to worry about (*insert fear*) anymore because you know you can experience the passing of time any way you want to do – fast or slow. But it is not only (*insert fear*) you can handle so well – being calm and confident in that situation. You know you can handle any difficult situation you might have to face in the future.

Your clock can also help you to enjoy and remember happy times. Maybe right now you would like to think of a time when you were really happy – just imagine it. Remember what you were doing and what you enjoyed most about it. As you are enjoying the memory – thinking about what you were doing – remember what you were thinking – what you were feeling inside. Imagine your clock. You need to slow time down to enjoy the happy time and experience those lovely feelings again. See the big hand – and slow it down as you know how to do. Then see the small hand – and slow it down as you know how to do. By taking control and slowing down time you can enjoy your happy time over and over again.

You are ready now to slow time down anytime you want when you are enjoying happy times in the future – you can make happy times and good feelings last longer using your clock.

Chapter 15

Going back in time

Introduction

Regression techniques can be used in hypnotherapy to find the root cause of a problem and this can be helpful to resolve a wide range of issues. Not all hypnotherapists favour or use regression techniques; many prefer to utilise solution-focussed therapy or cognitive behavioural therapy. Hypnotherapists also have varying views as to whether Past Life Regression should be used with children. Those who do use it with children (including myself) believe it can be effective with children aged seven upwards.

There are other scripts in this book that include regression techniques, but I wanted to include the two scripts below specifically for those hypnotherapists who want to use regression to regress a child. Sometimes the hypnotherapist will want to regress to a specific incident, at other times the script can be used to let the subconscious lead the way to whatever needs to be dealt with. This could be an incident(s) which has happened in the child's current life, but the hypnotherapist should always be prepared for the possibility that a child will sometimes regress to a past life. It is important to go with whatever happens, using some questions and prompts without leading the child in any way.

Script 1: The castle and drawbridge

It might be good to go back to see what happened (*insert event*) and maybe learn something about what happened and why it made you feel a certain way. You may feel differently about it afterwards.

I want you to imagine you see in the distance a big old medieval castle. I wonder if you are seeing different parts of the castle – towers – turrets – look-out places. The castle is surrounded by a moat – a big ditch filled with water. The castle has a big drawbridge that lifts up and down so people can come in and out of the castle. Just focus your attention on the drawbridge. Watch it drop down – very very slowly and stop. Then watch it lift up – very very slowly until it is closed. Watch again. The drawbridge is dropping down – very very slowly and then it stops. Now watch it lift up – very very slowly and it is closed.

The castle is a very interesting place to visit so I think you might enjoy going inside and having a look around. To do that though you need to get the drawbridge to lower again. So focus your special mind and tell the drawbridge to drop down – very very slowly. Watch it drop – very very slowly. Tell me when it has stopped.

Walk towards the drawbridge and stand at the edge. Take some gentle breaths and when you are ready, start to walk across the drawbridge. You might be feeling very curious – wondering what you might find inside the castle. Tell me when you have crossed over the drawbridge and you are ready to enter the castle and go into the courtyard.

So in you go. There is a courtyard right in front of you. Look for the soldiers in their armour who are there to protect the castle and keep people safe when they enter the castle. You may see some horses which have been tied up whilst their owners have gone inside the castle. There may be some other livestock too: pigs – cows – sheep – hens, and other traders selling their goods.

Now cross over the courtyard and go into the castle. You find yourself standing on a corridor. The corridor stretches far into the distance. The floor and walls are made of stone, which has been there since the castle was built a very long time ago. The stone is rock solid – safe and secure. The stone makes the castle very safe and secure, so as you are thinking about the stone, you feel safe and secure in the castle and on this corridor.

Now this particular corridor is very special because as you walk along it you can go back in time and see what happened.

As you walk down the corridor you are drifting back in time – remembering all sorts of things. People you have met; places you have been; things you have done.

Just keep drifting back and back. Going back in time. The corridor has a way of getting you to the place you need to be…

Do you know how old you are?
Look down and see what you are wearing.
Can you smell anything?
Can you hear anything?
Is anybody else there?
What are you doing?
How do you feel?
What happens next?

(Guidance note: be prepared for the fact that a child may go back to a past life and describe images/people from another lifetime/society)

Script 2: The train

I want you to imagine that you are standing outside a very old train station. There are lots of people around you. Some are in a hurry – walking very quickly. Others are taking their time – just sauntering along. Some people have luggage and are going somewhere on a journey; others are just hanging about waiting to meet someone. There are all sorts of noises around as well – from the traffic, the people, the trains, buses, taxis and aeroplanes in the sky. What else can you see? What else can you hear?

Now it is time to go into the train station. Can you see an entrance or is there more than one entrance? When you are ready just go in. You will see even more people hurrying and walking about. People who work in the station and people who work on the trains. Passengers and their friends or relatives ready to wave them goodbye. Just have a walk around and see what else you can see.

Now this is a very old train station and the trains are very old too. They are all steam trains. A steam train runs on coal and has a fire burning inside to make it go fast. It also has a water tank, a boiler, a cistern, a piston and right on top a chimney for the steam to come out and blow high into the air.

How many platforms can you see? I want you to find the steam train that is going to leave in a short while. First of all you need to go and buy a ticket to travel back in time. So find the ticket office and get your ticket. Then go to the platform where the train is waiting.

How many carriages does the train have? Go and have a look in each one. Find one which is empty and one which you would like to travel in. Off you go – have a good look – take your time. So which carriage are you going to travel in? OK – so get into the empty carriage and find yourself a seat by a window. Make yourself very comfortable and relaxed. Now you are ready to start your journey.

Now the strange thing about this train is that when it travels it looks as though it is going forward but in fact it is going backwards. It is a train that travels backwards in time. I want you to look out of the window as it is starting to set off from the train station. As you look out of the window you will see people, trains, other parts of the train station. You might hear different noises coming from the train – the wheels turning on the railway tracks.

Now just relax and as the train leaves the station and starts the journey back in time, look out of the window and you will start to see times from your life passing by the window. You are going backwards – travelling backwards through your life. Tell me what you are seeing.

Now the train knows when you need to stop and talk about things that have happened. You are not worried about this because you know you have to think about things and maybe see them in a different way. You can do this in two different ways. If you want you can look at things that have happened from the safety of your seat in the carriage – just look out through window. Or you can get out off the train and jump back into whatever you were looking at through the window.

Now the train knows exactly when to stop. It will start to slow down and your life outside the window will start to slow down until you just see one situation. Tell me when the train has stopped. Now tell me what you are seeing. Do you want to stay in your seat or get off the train and jump into the situation?

(Guidance note: the hypnotherapist should then help the child to talk about what they are seeing through the window if they want to stay in their seat, or encourage the child to relive the experience by being in the situation if s/he has chosen to get off the train)

Chapter 16

Star in the sky

Introduction

This is another script which can be used as a general introduction to trance and relaxation, but in addition it can be used specifically to create a safe place for the child. The star becomes somewhere they can relax and feel at peace.

This script has proven to be useful to pupils/students who are tired, feeling lethargic and lacking motivation for studying, revision or exams. The star can help them relax when they need to do so but it can also give them a boost of whatever they need (e.g. energy, enthusiasm, confidence).

I have included several additional scripts which can be used after the main script has helped the child find their own star. The child can explore further afield by exploring the moon using the first additional script. This is good to use in a first session to demonstrate the power of the imagination.

If a child has sleeping difficulties the script 'Swinging to Sleep' will help them get to sleep or get them back to sleep if they wake up in the middle of the night.

There is also an additional script for younger children who are bereaved and maybe do not understand the concept of death as an adult would know it. Many children are told their loved one is now a star in the sky. The script takes the child on another journey to find the star of the person who has died. The child can then talk to the person who has passed.

The script

It can be fun to go off to new and exciting places, and your special mind is there to help you do this anytime you want. That is why you have been given a great imagination. So let's see where you can go right now. Just make yourself comfortable. It does not matter whether you keep your eyes open or if you choose to rest them by closing them. Do whatever feels right for you.

Just imagine that it is night-time and you are outside somewhere lying on your back – looking up at the beautiful dark clear sky. The sky looks dark, smooth and velvety – a bit like a large slab of dark chocolate. There are little sparkles dotted all over the sky – sparkles that flash on and off. You realise that these are the stars – shining so brightly.

And can you see the moon? The moon hides sometimes. It hides behind clouds so you cannot see it at all or at other times it only shows half of itself. What is the moon doing tonight? Can you see anything else in the sky?

It would be fun to take a journey up towards the sky – to see the stars and moon up close. So you choose how you want to travel up there – how are you going to do it? OK then – when you are ready – off you go. Travel slowly and gently up into the sky. Making good progress – going higher and higher – up and up. Getting nearer and nearer to the stars. Look around you as you go. Enjoy every moment of this journey. Tell me what you see.

As you get near to the stars, start watching out for a special star – one which shines much brighter than all the others. It is shining so brightly to let you know where it is and that it is your star. So go on – go and find your star. You may have to travel around the other stars before you find your star. Weaving in and weaving out – moving up and moving down. Just take your time. Enjoy looking at all the stars and sparkles around you. Take as much time as you like and enjoy being in the sky – in the dark, smooth and velvety darkness. Keep looking for your star and let me know when you find it.

So now go a little closer to your star. Stars have points – some have five points; others may have more – six, seven or even eight. Look at your star – how many points does it have? Feel the light and energy coming from your star to greet you. Light and energy surrounds you – this is such a good feeling. You can use that positive energy anytime you want in the future; it is there to help you in any way you want – to help with your thoughts, feelings and behaviours (*or insert a specific issue e.g. concentration, motivation, studying, learning*).

Remember the star is full of light and energy. Anytime you feel tired and you need a boost of energy, all you have to do is say '*energy*' and you will feel that boost rush through your whole body very quickly. Just try that now – say '*energy*'.

When you are ready – go and explore your star. Maybe you would like to climb up to the points and see what the view is like from each one. After you have had a good look round your star just sit for a while and enjoy being on your star. You feel perfectly relaxed and peaceful. Remember this feeling.

Look around you – at the beautiful dark, smooth and velvety darkness; the sparkling stars – and the moon. The moon is so near you feel you could almost touch it. You can come to your star anytime you need a boost of energy or just to relax or it can take you anywhere you want to go – because your star is a shooting star and can get you to all sorts of places very quickly – all you have to do is say '*star*'.

(*Guidance note: the hypnotherapist can choose the alternative ways to proceed at this point depending what they need to work on*)

Additional script 1: Exploring the moon

Now I wonder if you would like to explore further and perhaps go for a walk on the moon. When you are ready decide how you are going to make your way to the moon and off you go. Tell me when you have landed there. Now just go and explore. What does it feel like being on another planet? What do you see around you? What is the temperature like? Is anyone or anything there? Go and explore some more – tell me what you find as you walk on the moon.

Additional script 2: Swinging to sleep

Now just find a comfortable spot on your star and lie down. Feel yourself sinking into your star, which is so very soft and comfortable. Just sink and sink, getting more and comfortable, ready to go to sleep. You feel a gentle movement as your star starts to swing slowly and gently. Your star is going to swing you gently to sleep. Feel it swing to the right – to the left – and back again. To the right – to the left – and back again.

Now as you are gently swinging to sleep, look above you – into the dark, smooth and velvety darkness. Look deep into the dark, smooth and velvety darkness. If you see any stars still sparkling look at them and start turning them off one by one. Do that now – turn the sparkling stars off one by one – and as you do this the dark, smooth and velvety darkness becomes even darker. You are feeling very very sleepy as your star keeps swinging you to sleep. Your eyelids are getting heavier and heavier as you drift off to sleep. Feeling sleepy and safe. Not thinking about anything at all. Just feeling sleepy and safe.

During the night if anything happens to wake you up (*insert if something regularly wakes the child e.g. nightmare; itching; a particular noise or sound*), then you can imagine being on your star and swing gently back to sleep. Feel your star swing to the right – to the left – and back again. To the right – to the left – and back again. Your eyelids are getting heavier and heavier as you drift back to sleep. Feeling sleepy and safe. Not thinking about anything at all. Just feeling sleepy and safe.

Additional script 3: Looking for the spiritual star

Now you know where your special star is and you can come here at any time. Everyone has a star somewhere in the sky – it is a place where a person can be happy and feel safe. I know you have been sad recently because (*insert name of person who has died*) has gone away. (*Name of person*) will have a special star of their own and it will shine brightly in the sky at night. Would you like to go and find that star now? As you have done before, decide how you are going to travel and start your journey to find (*name of person*)'s star. Weaving in and out – moving up and moving down. Look for (*name of person*)'s star. You will know when you see it. Take your time – tell me when you have found (*name of person*)'s star.

Can you tell me what (*name of person*)'s star is like? Do you want to go and sit on it?

Now that you are on this star can you see or feel (*name of person*) around you? Is there anything you would like to say to (*name of person*)? Is there anything you would like to do with (*name of person*)?

(Guidance note: the hypnotherapist can encourage the child to talk to the person and deal with any unresolved issues if there are any)

This is such a lovely star. It shines brightly and it is a very peaceful place to be. (*Name of person*) will be able to rest here, but the really good thing is s/he will be able to see down to earth and see what you are doing – at home, school (*insert other places, activities the child does*). S/he will not miss a thing because s/he will be able to see with the star shining so brightly and s/he will always be with you.

It works the other way too. With the star shining so brightly you can look up to the sky at night and know that (*name of person*) is there – watching you from their star.

Chapter 17

Harry the heron

Introduction

Harry was one of the first animals I saw when I moved into my current therapy room. Herons are so graceful and it is amazing for how long they can stand perfectly still. Humans could learn a lot from Harry, that is, how important and rewarding it is to take time out and look at the beautiful surroundings. Children love to watch Harry and so it was essential that I write a script about him.

The script can be used as a simple introduction to trance and as a deepener. It is especially effective when working with children who are deemed to be hyperactive or have difficulty with concentration.

I have inserted some questions into the script so the hypnotherapist can choose whether they want to engage the child more, or it can be simply read as a guided script to get the child into a deep trance state.

The script

Harry is a grey heron who has lived on the island in a big city all his life. A river runs through the city and Harry likes to spend as much time as he can by the river, either standing in it or flying high above it. He is a very majestic, elegant bird who walks up and down the river proudly each day but he also flies high above the trees.

Everything about Harry is long – very very long, which makes him exceptionally graceful.

Like all grey herons Harry has a very long yellow bill, so he can snap up lots of his favourite food very quickly and from quite a long way away. He loves to eat fish, small birds and wriggly insects.

Harry has a beautiful long slim neck, which goes into an S shape whenever he flies, whilst his long long legs stretch right out beneath his body.

Harry's head and body are covered in beautiful long, smooth grey feathers. Harry is very proud of his feathers and uses his bill to keep them neat and tidy. His bill is also good for scratching whenever he gets an itch in his feathers. Harry likes to keep himself looking good. One of his favourite sayings is: 'Look good on the outside and feel good on the inside'.

Harry has huge wings to help him fly. They actually stretch out to six feet and help him to fly very fast when he needs to get somewhere quickly or to go at a slower pace whenever he wants to just fly about to relax. His wings do whatever is right for him at the time. What Harry is really good at is being still. He likes nothing better than standing in the water on the river and just gazing out in front of him. He can do this for hours and hours and hours on end.

Harry is a bird of routine. Early in the morning he likes to stand in a particular part of the river under the huge trees and he looks across to the riverbank where his nest is hidden. At lunchtime he changes position and goes to a point where he looks down the river – looking far away into the distance. In the afternoon he tends to change his position again. When he stands in the river Harry likes to be still – very very still.

I wonder if you would like to imagine that you are a heron. Have you ever wondered what it is like to fly? What would it feel like? Well – Harry lives in a nest which is very high up in a tree located back from the river on the riverbank. Just imagine you are in your very own nest – feeling warm and safe. Take a look out from the nest and look up to the sky. How does it look? It's time to take a trip up into the sky. So take a few nice deep breaths and when you are ready take off – up you go.

Spread those huge wings and flap away – up, up and up you go. Higher and higher; feeling lighter and lighter. What do you see below you? How are you feeling as you go higher and higher? Make yourself fly faster. Now slow down. You can do anything you want: go fast, go slow, change direction – go to wherever you want to be.

Now after all that flying maybe you would like to take a walk in the river to wind down a bit and just relax. So when you are ready just fly down and down towards the river and land gently, very gently on the riverbank. Take a few, slow deep breaths and when you are ready slowly walk into the water – stretching out those long, long legs. Take your time. Walk slowly – there is no rush. Just enjoy the feeling of the cool water going up your legs as you go further into the river.

I wonder what you are seeing around you. Perhaps there are other birds or animals. Can you see any fish in the river – swimming below the surface of the water? Can you hear anything? I wonder which way you are going to go for a nice gentle walk in the river. You decide and when you are ready just walk – stretch out those long, long legs. Slow your breathing down as you walk along the river.

Good – you are feeling calm and relaxed as you walk further and further down the river. Enjoy the feeling of being relaxed. I wonder if you can become even more relaxed. Herons are so good at standing still and gazing in front of them for hours and hours and hours. Why don't you try to see how long you can just stand and gaze?

Find a spot in the river where you feel peaceful. Take your time – find that spot. Then make yourself comfortable – focus on the different parts of your body and relax each part one at a time. Where would you like to start? The tip of your long bill? Your head? Your wings? Your legs? Wherever suits you best. Just feel each part relax and become floppy. That's very good.

Think about your feathers. You have so many beautiful feathers. Feel each feather relax completely. As your feathers are relaxing one by one so you become more and more still. Now look in front of you. Just let your mind drift and drift. Let your imagination go anywhere it wants to go while you stand so still in the river…

Chapter 18

Bertie the beagle

Introduction

Bertie the beagle is like many young children: he gets overexcited, can be very loud and forgets about how he might make other people feel. So children who have behaviour problems will be able to relate to Bertie and the fact that he gets told off a lot. The script explains how Bertie learns to change his behaviour and what the benefits are to him and his family in the long run.

The benefits approach, which Roy Hunter[1] developed from the work of his teacher and mentor Charles Tebbetts, is used by many hypnotherapists when working with adults, but I think it can be a useful approach to adopt for children. A child is likely to be more motivated to work on changing their behaviour if they can see a benefit to them rather than focussing on the desires of others (e.g. parents, teachers). Therefore, I think it is helpful to do some preparatory work with the child talking about 'benefits' but using a term which is meaningful and age-appropriate for them. Basically, it is finding out what they can gain from changing their behaviour i.e. what is in it for them.

Doing the work on benefits can be done in the conscious state or in the trance state. If done in the conscious state, the child can come up with a list of benefits which the hypnotherapist can then use when undertaking the therapeutic work in trance.

The script tells the story of Bertie, who does benefit from changing his behaviour (as do other people). The hypnotherapist can follow on from this story by asking the child what behaviours s/he would like to change and how this would benefit them.

The script

I don't know how much you know about beagles but they are one of the oldest breeds of dogs to live in England. They have been living here for thousands of years. They lived here even when the Roman Empire existed – that's a long long time ago. I know a beagle called Bertie, who used to be so naughty when he was a puppy; he is much better behaved nowadays. Perhaps you would like to imagine what Bertie looks like.

Bertie has lots of white fur on his body – some on his handsome face, tummy, legs and paws. He also has brown and black bits; some are on his face, others on his floppy long ears and he also has some on his back. Now Bertie is a purebred beagle – he came from a long line of special beagles and even has the paperwork which shows his family tree. Now purebred beagles always have some white in their tail. Bertie has a white tip right at the end of his tail. Can you see it?

Beagles have very good noses and they can smell things that other people can't. Bertie's nose is very black and so shiny. Bertie loves to sniff and smell things; he really likes to put his nose to the ground and follow a smell.

The word 'beagle' in French means 'loudmouth' and Bertie certainly is very good at barking and howling. He can make a lot of noise.

Bertie had been born on a farm in the country where pedigree beagles were bred. A young couple came to look at the newest litter of puppies when they were born, and as soon as they saw Bertie they wanted him. They had to wait some weeks before they could take him home with them. When the day came to leave the farm, Bertie was sad to leave his mum, brothers and sisters but at the same time he was very excited about seeing his new home. He was going to live with the couple and their two cats, Betsey and Coco, in a newly built house.

Bertie got so excited exploring in his new home. He started sniffing every corner in every room. He pulled things out of cupboards and drawers. The more excited he got the more he ran around sniffing. Sometimes he even ran round in circles chasing his own tail. He got so giddy.

The couple thought Bertie was getting overexcited because everything was new to him and they expected him to calm down after a few weeks. This did not happen. Bertie did some very naughty things – even when the couple kept telling him not to. He would jump on things. He chased the cats and also stole their food. He chewed shoes, slippers and socks – anything he could get his paws on really. He even bit off parts of the garden fence. He really was a naughty beagle.

Helen the hypnotherapist did not advertise the fact that she sometimes helped animals using hypnosis. Both people and animals do talk, so animals would go to see Helen when they needed some help with something. At other times Helen would hear things or be told things. She did hear that the young couple were having problems with their new beagle's behaviour.

So Helen went so see the couple and said she had heard they were having a few difficulties with their new puppy. She offered to take Bertie out on a few walks to get to know him. Helen did not know what she had let herself in for. Even though Bertie was only a puppy it was like he was taking Helen for a walk not the other way round. He was very strong and quick. Once they set off his nose was to the ground and he was sniffing away. He loved smelling rubbish on the street; as soon as he smelt a can of pop or a takeaway box he was off, dragging Helen behind him.

Bertie also became very loud when he was outdoors. Whenever he saw children or other dogs he would get very excited and bark very loudly for minutes on end; it was almost deafening. This frightened a lot of people because Bertie's bark was so loud and it sounded so very fierce. Bertie also liked to run and jump up at children and other dogs, which again was a little bit scary for some of them. Bertie was just being friendly.

Helen was exhausted after their first walk and said to Bertie: "It is lovely that you are so curious and have got so much energy but you need to control how you behave. I want you to think about certain situations when you need to calm down and I am going to teach you how to breathe to help you. You are very good at smelling but let's see if you can improve your breathing".

Bertie was a bit puzzled because he thought he was pretty good at breathing already, but was willing to give it a go if it meant him not getting told off so much by everyone.

Helen said:

> Just breathe in very slowly and gently while I count to 3 and then gently out for 3. Don't gulp air – try to control it. OK – now breathe in *1, 2, 3* and hold – and now out – *3, 2, 1*. That's good.

Bertie was quite proud of himself as he found this quite easy, but he also realised he was starting to feel a bit sleepy after he had done it a few times. He felt very calm indeed. Helen said he should try and practise his breathing at least four times a day in order to keep *calm*.

Helen kept using the word '*calm*' and suggested that when they went out walking if Bertie got a bit overexcited she would say the word '*calm*' to him so he would know to slow down and practise his breathing.

Bertie did practise his breathing and after a few more walks, Helen told Bertie that he was really very good at both smelling and breathing, so she suggested that he try breathing in and out for *4*:

> Just breathe in very slowly and gently while I count to 4 and then gently out for 4. Don't gulp air – try to control it. OK – now breathe in *1, 2, 3, 4* and hold – and now out – *4, 3, 2, 1*. That's good.

Bertie continued to practise his breathing every day and over the next few months he felt so much calmer and his behaviour got so much better. He could do all the things he enjoyed related to smelling and finding things, but he could also control his behaviour when he felt he was getting overexcited. He had learnt to respect other people's feelings and their belongings.

Bertie is now fully grown and a very well-behaved beagle who lives happily and contentedly with the young couple and the two cats. If you asked him what were the benefits of changing his behaviour, he would say first of all it is so good not to be told off all the time. The cats seem to like him now; they even come and snuggle up to him on the sofa. People in the park who admire his shiny nose, long ears and white-tipped tail, come up and stroke him. So all in all, life is much better.

So now shall we think about what behaviours you might like to change and what the benefits might be?

(Guidance note: the hypnotherapist can then proceed to work with the child in making changes using the benefits approach)

Note

1 Hunter, C.R (2011) *The Art of Hypnotherapy*. Bancyfelin, Carmarthen: Crown House Publishing Ltd.

Chapter 19

Chinga the cat

Introduction

There are so many techniques that a hypnotherapist can use but it is always important to find the best way to work with a client. Some hypnotherapists do not believe that regression techniques should be used with a child; they feel solution-focussed techniques are more appropriate. I do use regression with some children, and mixed with a metaphor it can work very well.

In my own practice I like to find the root cause of a problem and release it. Regression techniques facilitate this methodology and can be used for a wide range of problems. In the script which follows, Chinga the cat had developed a fear of needles after a bad experience at the vet's when she was a kitten. Regression is used by Helen the hypnotherapist to release the feelings and fears which have developed for Chinga over the years.

This script can be adapted to find out the root cause of other fears or phobias a child may be experiencing, but obviously would not be suitable if the child had a phobia or fear about a cat.

The script

Chinga is a beautiful tabby cat with four very white paws, who lives with her husband, Charles, who is a ginger cat. They live and work in a place called the Tiger Works, which is a huge old industrial building which is now divided into little workshops which are rented out to all sorts of different people. The Tiger Works is owned by Mr and Mrs Snaith. Mrs Snaith loves cats and does a lot of voluntary work for the local Cat Protection Society. Mr Snaith is not so keen on cats as their fur causes him to sneeze.

Mr and Mrs Snaith bought Chinga and Charles to work in the Tiger Works, which is close by a river, to ensure that no mice or rats got into the workshops. The cat couple are very good at their jobs. During the past three years Chinga has had many litters of kittens; sometimes there have been up to five kittens in a litter which has been exhausting for her. Some of the kittens have been given jobs to do in the Tiger Works; others have gone to live at the homes of people working in the Tiger Works. Mrs Snaith has also found good homes through the Cat Protection Society. However, the day came when Mr Snaith said to his wife: "Enough is enough; Chinga needs to have an operation to stop her having any more kittens".

Mrs Snaith told Chinga that she was going to take her to the vet's next week. From that moment on Chinga felt sick and terrified. "Why?" you might ask. Well it was because she had always had a fear of needles since being a kitten herself. She had had a very bad experience with a vet. She does not like watching any of those hospital programmes on the television. She has to turn her head away if she sees a needle – even if it is just on the television. If anyone talks about the needles, she immediately starts to feel sick.

The day after being told about the operation Chinga just could not concentrate on her work. She felt sick; her legs felt wobbly and she kept getting very hot under her fur and the collar around her neck. Charles knew what the matter was and said "I think you need to go and see Helen the hypnotherapist", who worked in one of the workshops in the Tiger Works. Chinga knew that Helen often worked late into the evening, so that night she waited outside Helen's door. As Helen was saying 'good-bye' to her last client of the day, she saw Chinga sitting on the doormat. Helen loved cats so she asked Chinga to come in and sit on her lap.

Chinga told Helen about the operation and how scared she was of needles. Helen smiled and said: "Well I am sure I can help you, but you will need to practise relaxing every day until you go to the vet's". Chinga said she really wanted to get rid of her fear and promised to practise relaxing every day. Helen asked Chinga to go and sit on the chair opposite to where she was sitting and began talking to Chinga:

> Now just close your eyes and breathe in and out very slowly and gently. That's right. Good. Now when you are worried about something, it is good to try to think about something else so you are not thinking about the thing that is worrying you. Now I know that you are worried about going to the vet's again because you had a bad experience some years ago. Let's see if we can rid of that for you.
>
> So just keep breathing nice and slowly. The day is drawing to an end – you have done all your work for today, so just relax. Just slow your breathing down – breathe in a wave of relaxation and breathe out anything you don't want. Just feel the relaxation going through every bit of your beautiful tabby fur and your four white paws relax as well. That's good. You even feel the whiskers on your face relax, and your mouth opens slightly and your tongue relaxes. That's good.
>
> Just let your mind drift – let it drift to a place where you feel really safe and comfortable. Where might that be?

Chinga responded: I love to go and sit underneath the big boiler that heats the whole of the Lion Works. It is so warm there. I took an old blanket I found that someone had thrown out and put it under the pipes. I can snuggle down and no-one knows I am there. I can get away from everything. It is so peaceful.

Helen said: That sounds like a really good safe place for you. So you can go there in your imagination too at any time just to feel safe and peaceful. All you have to do is put your two front paws together so they are touching. Do that now.

Now that you are feeling so relaxed, I want you to imagine that you are walking over the old bridge on the river and as you are doing this the bridge is taking you back in time. Keep walking – going back in time – back in time to when you were at the vet's. The bridge is sturdy and safe so you can do this – go back in time and see the room in the vet's surgery.

Now for a short time remember what happened. Look at the room you are in. Remember being ready for the operation. The vet preparing to put you to sleep – getting the injection ready.

Now as Helen the hypnotherapist was talking, Chinga went back in her mind to when she had the bad experience. Chinga remembered everything and she started to shake with fright. Helen reminded Chinga that she could go to her safe place at any time by putting her two front paws together and said to her 'Just stay with it for now if you can, Chinga. Remember exactly what the vet did.'

Whilst Chinga was remembering she told Helen that the vet suddenly stuck the needle in her side without saying what he was going to do. It was such a shock and she jumped, so the needle hurt her badly. The vet had to take the needle out and put it in again. Then suddenly she was asleep. After the operation when she woke up, Chinga felt very sore where the vet had put in the needle.

Helen said to Chinga: 'You were very young when this happened. You are much older now – an adult cat who has had lots of litters of kittens. Remember that memory now and this time remember it as a grown-up cat. What would you have said to the vet?'

Chinga said exactly what she would have wanted to happen before she had the needle put in her side. She wanted the vet to explain what was going to happen – where was the needle to go in exactly. She wanted him to tell her to look away just before he was going to insert the needle. She wanted him to put the needle in very gently. Helen asked her to imagine this not just once but twice and then a third time. Each time Chinga imagined it she felt so much better.

Helen the hypnotherapist told Chinga that she knew what she needed to do when she went to the vet's in a few days' time for the operation and that it would be good to imagine and rehearse what she was going to say over the next few days. She then asked Chinga to imagine she was walking back over the old bridge into the present time and back into her workshop. Chinga opened her eyes and felt so calm and peaceful.

Helen explained it had been good for Chinga to remember and then get rid of the bad feelings that came with the memory, but she also now knew what she was going to say to the vet when she went for her operation in a few days' time. Chinga practised her breathing every day before she was taken to the vet's, and on the morning of the operation she felt calm and relaxed.

You'll be glad to know the operation went well and everyone was happy – especially Mr Snaith who was very glad that Chinga was not going to have any more litters of kittens.

Chapter 20

The salmon triplets

Introduction

This script tells the story of the salmon triplets who could not stop scratching themselves and each other. The scratching was a way of dealing with a physical condition but it had become a habit. Many children scratch or itch either out of habit or because they have a condition such as eczema. The hypnotherapist might want to do some work on an actual condition, which is related to stress or anxiety, but the main objective of this script is to work on stopping the habit. I have found the script has been very effective in helping children with particular skin problems, but it can also be used as a metaphor to address other habits e.g. thumb-sucking.

The script

I want to tell you about a river which has lots of special fish in it – some of which are salmon. People who like to go fishing are not allowed to fish at certain times of the year and they cannot fish without a licence.

One year there was a salmon who had triplets, but they were born with a certain condition that made their skin and scales very itchy. It was very irritating for the three of them and their mum got fed up telling them not to scratch. She felt very bad about this, because it sounded like she was always nagging them. You see the triplets were very good at scratching each other. Salmon have a big tail fin at the back of them, but they also have a lot of fins around the top and bottom of their body. So they used to tell each other when they were itchy and they would use their fins to scratch each other.

The scratching would ease the itching for a bit, but it did not really help. In fact, it actually made things worse as the triplets' skins and protective scales got damaged and started to bleed.

An older, very wise salmon, Samuel, heard about the triplets' problem and came to talk to them; their mum was there as well. He said he had had the same problem when he was a young salmon and someone called Danny the dolphin had helped him by asking him to imagine certain things. He asked the triplets' mum if she would like him to help the triplets. Mum was more than grateful. So they all positioned themselves in the river and got comfortable. Samuel said:

> Close your eyes and imagine that you have travelled to a beautiful beach on a desert island far far away. Now when you are imagining you can make anything

happen and imagine that you can do things that you would not normally be able to do. So imagine that you are walking perhaps on your tail fin along the beach – just relaxing – and you are going to go for a swim. When you are ready just get in the beautiful clear, blue sea. It is warm and comforting. Now swim out deeper into the sea.

As you swim out you see some dolphins playing and having fun. One of the dolphins comes towards you and introduces himself: 'Hello I'm Danny. I was expecting you. I hear you have itchy skin and scales. I think I can help with that'.

Danny asks you to swim alongside him and takes you far out into the sea. He says you are going to a special part of the sea that has healing powers. As you nearly reach the special part of the sea you start to feel that your skin and scales feel a bit different. As you go into the special part of the sea you feel your skin and scales stop itching completely. Your skin feels smooth as the special waters wash all over your body – soothing and healing – taking all the itchiness away.

Danny says that you can swim to this special part of the sea anytime you want for some healing from the waters. He then asks you to dive down to the bottom of the seabed. Do that now. Look at all the wonderful things you can see: different coloured fish; other creatures; objects that have been thrown into the sea. Danny asks you to find some seaweed – go and have a look for that now and bring it back to him.

Danny says this is very special seaweed. Like the special part of the sea, it has powers to heal. So just imagine that your skin and scales are itching again. Now rub the seaweed all over your skin and feel the itching stop. Feel your skin become smooth and see how good it looks.

So that is how Danny the dolphin helped me to stop scratching my skin. You know now you can come into the sea at any time you are itchy and look for Danny the dolphin yourself. He will help you too by swimming with you to the special part of the sea where the healing waters are or you can swim directly to the bottom of the sea to find the seaweed to rub on your skin and scales.

The three of you will not scratch each other any more. If one of you ever gets itchy and asks to be scratched the other two will say: 'Sea'.

So the triplets did start using their imaginations and in the next few days went to the special part of the sea quite a few times each day, but as the days went on they needed to go less and less because they were itching and scratching less and less. Until finally they did not itch or scratch at all.

Chapter 21

Maurice the mole

Introduction

There are many children who are deemed to be 'loners'; often they just enjoy their own company but this is seen as being 'odd' or 'not normal'. Children have the right to be respected for who they are as individuals and their uniqueness. Maurice the mole has a lot to teach both children and adults about enjoying solitude.

This script is aimed at children who enjoy their own company, but maybe have experienced ridicule, been made fun of because they do spend a lot of time on their own. The key message in the story is that it is perfectly fine to enjoy your own company. The issue of image and how people make assumptions, which are often incorrect, is also addressed.

The script will also prove useful to children who have become isolated – not through their own choice. They may find socialising, making friends difficult or they have been subjected to bullying, experienced being ridiculed, mocked or mimicked. Whatever the reason, the script will help the child to be resourceful.

Maurice's story also explores strategies of what to do when feeling panicky or frightened; the use of breathing exercises and mantras are included. The story is about being resourceful and using the strengths you have.

Being a mole Maurice spends a lot of time underground and the script follows Maurice into his tunnels and chambers. Therefore, it is not appropriate to use this script with a child who does not like the dark or who is claustrophobic.

The script

Maurice the mole is often misunderstood. People think he is a rodent like a rat or a mouse and he is often labelled 'a nuisance'. They could not be more wrong. Maurice likes to be on his own and is really no trouble to anyone at all. Some people think it is odd to want to be on your own – but actually there is nothing wrong with that if you like your own company. Maurice is always polite to other animals if he comes across them but he does not really like talking very much. He likes to keep himself to himself.

Other things people get wrong about Maurice are that they think he is blind and has no ears. Well I'd like to tell you the truth about Maurice, because he is a very interesting, clever and determined little mammal. Before I do that, maybe you would like to imagine what he looks like.

Moles are covered in fur and not many people know that the fur can be black, white, cream, grey or even orange. Maurice has grey fur. Now moles spend most of their time in tunnels underground – they do not like being above the ground. As moles are in the dark a lot of the time their eyes often look like they are shut when they do come above ground. Maurice can see but not like you see things; his sight is a bit blurred. He cannot see any colours at all, but he is very good at telling the difference between dark and light.

As Maurice's sight is not one of his strengths other parts of his body have been made in special ways to help him. Instead of having a nose like yours which is short and placed neatly on your face, Maurice has a very long – exceedingly long in fact – snout which makes him really good at breathing and smelling. Maurice loves to eat earthworms and when he is moving along tunnels his snout smells out the worms and other foods he likes.

Maurice is good at hearing things too. You can't see his tiny ears because they go inside his head rather than being on the outside. This is so soil does not get in his ears when he is digging to make tunnels in the earth. His tiny earholes are hidden by fur.

Now his earholes may be tiny but Maurice has two extra big paws which have long curved claws at the end. These claws are there to help Maurice dig down and down into the earth. Maurice is really fast at digging his way down into the earth and making new tunnels which he finds exciting as he likes to go to new places. He likes to think of the tunnels as 'Maurice's Highway of Tunnels' because they can take him anywhere he wants to go in the real world or in his imaginary world.

Moles like to live alone. On an acre of land you will only find two or maybe three moles living there. They rarely talk to each other but will always be polite if they happen to come across each other. They like minding their own business below the ground. The tunnels are warm, cosy and safe. I wonder if you would like to follow Maurice into his Highway of Tunnels.

So just imagine Maurice again. Look at his grey fur – his exceedingly long snout – his huge paws and claws – and his tail. I wonder if you were a mole what colour your fur would be.

When you are ready, imagine that you are starting to follow Maurice. His snout is sniffing around for the entrance to a tunnel. You see his snout go down into the ground and then you see his head disappear and then his whole body has gone. You better be quick and follow him. Moles move very very quickly.

Down you go – taking nice deep breaths – moving steadily down and down into the earth. Follow Maurice's tail. It is dark in the tunnel but not at all scary. If you look back up to the hole at the top of the entrance you can still see the blue sky and rays of sunshine. But you know you want to follow Maurice, so down you go. See how fast Maurice is travelling and feel the excitement about seeing where he lives. So down and down you go further into the tunnel. Feeling the speed and excitement about seeing how someone else lives their life, which may be quite different to your life. It is good to be different. Isn't this fun following Maurice?

As you go further and further down you realise that Maurice has built other tunnels off the main tunnel. You can explore these later if you want to but for now just follow Maurice because he is going to take you to the end of this main tunnel where he has built his 'special chambers'. That is mole language for 'rooms'. So just keep following Maurice until he stops.

Maurice is going to show you his chambers. The first one is the kitchen – just follow Maurice in there. See if you can find where Maurice stores the earthworms which he loves to eat.

The second chamber is where Maurice sleeps. He usually sleeps very well after a hard day of tunnelling but before drifting off to sleep he likes to imagine that he is going to places above ground – places he will never actually see but he knows that his imagination can take him to anywhere he wants to go.

Maurice has always fancied the idea of lying on a deserted beach and doing a bit of sunbathing. He knows he could never really do that because the sun would hurt his eyes and he would be too hot with all the fur that covers his body. But it is just nice to imagine. Another thing he would like to try is dancing – all different types of dancing. Imagine Maurice the mole dancing.

Although Maurice is very skilled at digging and making tunnels, he does sometimes come up against a problem. Sometimes the ground becomes very hard and frozen in winter and it takes much longer to get down into the earth. He is a very patient and determined mole so whenever this happens, he just keeps trying until he gets a breakthrough. Maurice is a mole who is full of determination, he never gives up. He says: 'Where there is a problem, there is always a solution'.

One winter Maurice was in the middle of digging a new tunnel when the snow started. He did not take much notice at first. The odd snowflake came into the tunnel but he just carried on. Maurice gets very involved in his work and when his claws are digging away Maurice goes into a relaxed dreamy state. After a while more and more snowflakes were appearing in the tunnel. Then when Maurice looked back he saw such brightness – behind him was so bright it hurt his small eyes. He came to realise that the tunnel was full of snow. He stretched his paws out to touch the snow – it was very cold. He decided that he would carry on digging for a while until the snow stopped as it usually did not last very long. But the snow did not stop falling that day – it went on and on and on. So Maurice decided to sleep in the new tunnel that night.

When Maurice woke the next morning the snow had come further down the tunnel and it had frozen. Maurice touched the iced snow – it was very very hard. So hard in fact even his sharp claws could not make a dent in it at all. Maurice suddenly felt very trapped and he started to feel a little bit anxious and panicky. This had never happened to him before. He took a few deep breaths and thought about what to do. At the same time saying to himself: 'Where there is a problem, there is always a solution'.

Maurice decided as he could not go backwards and get out of the tunnel he would just have to go forwards. He kept saying to himself: 'Going forwards is better than going backwards'. He planned to focus on his digging and making new chambers in order not think about the iced snow that was keeping him in this tunnel. So as he kept going forward Maurice imagined how he would decorate his new chambers and repeated to himself: 'Going forwards is better than going backwards'.

This turned out to be a very bad winter and the snow stayed for a very long time. Poor Maurice remained trapped in the new tunnel, but he did not let the situation get him down. On the odd occasion he did feel a bit panicky or scared when he heard strange noises above the ground, he would sit down and take slow deep breaths in through his very long snout and then take his time to gently breathe out. He finished his breathing exercises when he felt completely calm again and then he would often laugh to himself, because he was thinking about how some other animals had said his snout was far too long: 'If they were stuck down here they'd want a snout like mine to calm them down. My snout is so very good for breathing and making me feel relaxed'.

So Maurice kept calm and waited for the snow to melt. By which time he had dug several more tunnels and made some new chambers. He thought to himself: 'Some good always comes out of bad. I may have been a bit panicky and scared at times but there was no need really. I used my snout to breathe and keep me calm, and digging is always a good distraction. The good to come out of all this is I have more tunnels and new chambers'.

So it would seem that Maurice is a very resourceful mole; he uses all his strengths to help himself when he finds himself in a difficult situation.

Chapter 22

Harriet the hedgehog

Introduction

Being a victim of bullying is a problem for many children of all ages. It is not a new problem at all. We can all probably think of a child who was bullied when we were at school ourselves. Children can experience bullying in their own home or in the community. However, the problem seems to have extended further and bullying occurs in all sorts of places, for example via a phone or computer, text messages, emails, and can affect many aspects of a child's life. The development of social media has not helped and cyberbullying is being given a great deal of attention, although the statistics about incidence do differ tremendously.

The story of Harriet the Hedgehog explains how Harriet was rejected by her mum and bullied by her siblings. She was called many horrible things but one label in particular stayed with her – 'rubbish' – and she came to believe that she was this. This script will be of help to any child who has experienced any form of bullying, but also to children who have been abused and told by their perpetrator that they are 'worthless', 'stupid' or something else very negative which the child has come to believe is the truth. A hypnotherapist may also consider using this script for a child who has a physical disability and has experienced emotional harm from comments made about or to them.

It is very difficult for a child who has been bullied or abused to trust people after they have been harmed emotionally or physically. The script demonstrates that trust can be restored and that there are good people in the world. The script can be used to work on building self-esteem and confidence.

The script

I want to tell you about Harriet the hedgehog, because you remind me a bit of how Harriet used to be and I think you might like to know how things turned out for her.

I don't know if you know anything about hedgehogs but they are usually born in June or July or sometimes in the autumn. Baby hedgehogs are known as 'hoglets'. Once the babies are born the daddy hedgehog leaves the mummy hedgehog and he does not have much to do with bringing up the hoglets. Harriet and her three brothers were born in a park on a beautiful warm day in June. Harriet's mum, Hilda, had a difficult time giving birth to the hoglets; the three boys were born very quickly and close together, but it took hours and hours to get Harriet out. When she was being born,

Harriet's back right leg got stuck; it was twisted and then permanently damaged, so she always walked with a limp.

Hilda and her hoglets stayed in a warm, cosy nest for four weeks. Hilda was not very nice to her daughter because she could not forgive Harriet for the pain she had caused her during the birth. Hilda never cuddled Harriet and she was made to sleep on her own in the nest whilst Hilda slept with her three boy hoglets. The boy hoglets were cruel to Harriet; they bullied her and made fun of her damaged leg.

After a month Hilda started to take the hoglets out to learn how to find food so that they would be able to fend for themselves. Harriet could never keep up with her mum and brothers because of her leg. Hilda got angry with her daughter and shouted at her when she lagged behind. The boys laughed at Harriet and called her horrible names. After ten days Hilda said it was time for the hoglets to make their own way in life and she sent them on their way. Harriet was left all on her own. She walked about a bit but was very scared and started to cry. Hedgehogs don't like the daytime; they prefer to be out at night. So eventually she curled up into a tight ball to make herself feel safe and decided to wait for it to get dark before she walked any further.

During the early afternoon some boys were playing in the park and when they saw what looked like a round ball, they decided to have a game of football. They soon realised Harriet was not a ball and told her she was 'rubbish'. One boy then kicked Harriet towards the back of a big van which was parked near the entrance gates. Harriet landed in the back of the van where there were lots of parcels – all shapes and sizes. Some time passed and then the driver of the van shut the doors. The van began to move and this was very frightening for Harriet who did not understand what was happening. She kept rolling about in between all the parcels. She became very frightened again because did not know what all these strange shapes were and she was hearing sounds and noises she had never heard before. Harriet started to cry and just kept repeating to herself 'I'm rubbish'.

This van was delivering parcels to lots of different places. So the van kept stopping and starting; the driver kept opening and closing the doors. The parcels became fewer and fewer and eventually the van was completely empty. When the driver stepped into the van to make sure there were no parcels left, he saw the curled-up ball which was Harriet and picked her up. 'Who have we got here then?' asked the van driver, to which Harriet replied 'I'm rubbish'. 'I'm sure you're not. My name is Derek'.

Harriet told Derek how she had ended up in the back of his van. He seemed such a good listener that she told him all about how her mum and brothers had treated her and the names she had been called. Derek was worried about Harriet and thought she could do with staying with some kind people for a while. Derek knew a lot of the animals who lived in the area and was sure he could find someone who could help and support Harriet. So he carried Harriet down to the river and introduced her to Millicent Mouse, who had been through some rough times in her own life.

Millicent was more than happy to help Harriet: 'You can stay here for a couple of weeks, and then we need to find a nice garden for you to call your own'. Millicent invited other animals to come and meet Harriet, but she was very shy and often just curled up into a ball. She was not being rude; it was just her way of coping and she did not want people to see her leg.

Millicent told Harriet she needed to believe in herself and build up some confidence. Harriet said 'But I'm rubbish'. Millicent said: 'You most definitely are not "rubbish", my girl. Look at those beautiful spines on your back. They are absolutely gorgeous. How many have you got?' 'About 5,000' said Harriet.

Now Millicent knew from her own difficulties that it is important how you see yourself, but it is also important to protect yourself from people who are not nice to you and from the horrid and hurtful comments they might make. So Millicent suggested to Harriet:

> Just imagine that your spines are there to protect you. Close your eyes and imagine that you are looking at your beautiful spines. Now focus on one; look at the tip of it. Now start looking down from the tip of the spine – focussing on the different shades of brown on the spine. Slowly and gently. Feeling more and more relaxed. That's good. Now just look at all those spines – they are indeed very beautiful but they are also very sharp and are there to protect you – protect you from harm.
>
> So just for a moment remember some of the hurtful things that have been said to you. Maybe see those words, phrases, sentences flying towards you but see how they cannot get anywhere near you because the sharp spines keep you safe. The words, phrases, sentences just bounce off the spines and disappear completely. You can make those unkind things go away. Use your spines. After some time those unkind comments won't even to try to come near you. They can't hurt you anymore.
>
> Your spines are your protection – a bit like a blanket wrapped around you keeps you warm, comfortable and safe. Anytime in the future anybody says anything bad or hurtful to you just say 'spines' to yourself and imagine your spines protecting you from all those comments.

Well Harriet thought she would give this a try. So she started bringing into her mind all the things her mum and brothers had said to her. She said out loud some of the words and sentences when she was with Millicent, but she remembered more things when she was going to sleep at night. So over the next few days and nights she worked hard to remember all the things that had hurt her and got rid of them. She felt so much better and as she was feeling so much better, she did not roll up into a ball so often.

Millicent introduced Harriet to other animals who lived nearby. Harriet was still very shy but she was determined to get over this and talk to Millicent's friends. She just thought of her spines protecting her and she became more and more confident. One day she met Harry the Heron who asked if she knew about the allotment which was about a mile away. Harry had been thinking that this might be a good place for Harriet to settle.

So Harry the Heron and Millicent Mouse took Harriet to see the allotment. The three of them took a walk around. It was early morning so there were not too many humans about. They saw a lot of different things: sheds – garden tools which some people had forgotten to put away – vegetables – fruit – trees and flowers. It is such a lovely place. Harriet felt she had found home – she felt totally relaxed and at peace with herself.

Harry was very pleased that he had been able to help Harriet find a place where she could feel safe and comfortable and make a new start for herself. Millicent was very pleased too that she had been able to suggest that Harriet use her spines to get rid of bad things from the past. Harriet was so happy that she had her spines which were helping her to feel more and more confident every day.

(Guidance note: the hypnotherapist can then ask the child to think about how they can protect themselves, what they might use)

Chapter 23

Bees in the hives

Introduction

I think a hypnotherapist should be able to use a variety of techniques with children and not just follow one preferred method. Parts therapy[1] can be very effective with some adults and I believe it can work well with some children too. Parts therapy is taught on most hypnotherapy training courses, but I think a lot of practice is needed to develop the skill to use it effectively.

Parts therapy is based on the assumption that a person's personality/subconscious is made up of different parts and sometimes certain parts may be in conflict with each other – perhaps pulling in different directions when trying to achieve the same end. The hypnotherapist works with the subconscious to bring forward the part(s) which is/are hindering the achievement of goals. Work has to be undertaken to see whether the parts which are in conflict can work together i.e. resolve the inner conflict, or whether another part can come forward to help resolve the conflict.

It can get very complicated if the subconscious brings forward several parts. If a student or newly qualified hypnotherapist is interested in using parts therapy regularly, I think it is really helpful to do some more in-depth training for their Continued Professional Development (CPD).

As parts therapy can be complicated sometimes (but not always), when I wrote the script about the bees my aim was to develop something very simple which could be used to introduce a child to parts therapy. I think it is also a good way for a student and newly qualified hypnotherapist to develop their skills in using parts therapy.

Please note there is no such thing as a king bee in a hive; in the real world the only job of a male bee (drone) is to mate. I think it is absolutely fine to have a king bee in the imagination rather than a queen bee if the child introduces this – which boys often do.

Before using this script, the hypnotherapist should check out that the child does not have any bad memories of being stung by a bee or wasp.

The script

I want to tell you about the bees who lived in two beehives, which had been put in a very quiet spot near a river. So imagine the two hives having the perfect spot for the busy bees. Bees are such an important part of the local community and the world in general. They transfer pollen from between flowers and help plants grow. They also collect nectar from flowers to make honey. There are many beautiful flowers and plants on the two banks of the river. The flowers are so pretty in the summer – there are so many different colours. Can you see them?

Now I am not sure how much you know about bees and their hives. The queen bee is in charge and the lady bees do all the hard work. There are men bees too – they are known as drones. The lady bees fly in and out of their hive all day. They never stop working. What you might find funny is that they communicate with each other by dancing – they do what is called the 'waggle dance'. A beehive can have up to 50,000 bees living and working in it – imagine all those bees doing the waggle dance.

What is really interesting about bees is that they have very small brains – the size of a little seed – but they are absolutely brilliant at learning and remembering things. They can remember where flowers are and can report back to the queen bee.

The hives are made up of lots of different parts known as honeycombs. This is where the bees keep the pollen, nectar and honey. A beehive is a bit like your special mind, which is divided into parts; the hives are divided into honeycombs. A beehive never stops working and it produces lots of good things – just like the honey the bees make.

Imagine that your head is like a beehive but it's (*child's name*) hive. Go inside and see all the different honeycombs in (*child's name*) hive. Find the queen bee who is in charge – she is always in control. She knows what to do. She tells the bees what needs to be done in order to make good honey. Sometimes a few bees change the way they do things and they think they are helping at the time and doing their best, but actually they make things worse.

We have been talking about (*insert issue discussed*) and I think there may be a part of your special mind that has been trying to help you and it has done its best but some changes need to happen now to (*insert changes that the child wants to make*). So look around the different honeycombs in your hive. Find the honeycomb that has been working to help you but now needs to do things differently. Ask the bees in that honeycomb to come forward and talk to you.

Thank the bees for helping you. Then explain that some changes need to be made. Tell them what you want to happen in the future. Now ask them if they would like to help make some changes or do they feel it is time to retire and let some other bees help.

(Guidance note: the hypnotherapist needs to keep this simple for a young child but follow the process of parts therapy)

If the bees want to retire:

Thank the bees for helping you and wish them well in their retirement. Ask the queen bee which other bees could help you now with (*insert issue*) and to send them over to you. Greet the bees when they arrive. Explain what you want to happen (*insert changes*) and then ask them how they might help you.

If the bees want to continue:

Thank the bees for wanting to stay and help. Now tell them what you want them to do. Ask the queen bee if there are any other bees in other honeycombs that could help. If there are, ask her to send the bees over to you. Greet them when they arrive.

Ask the bees who have been working with you already if they are willing to work with the new bees. Then ask the new bees if they are willing to work with the bees who have been working with you already. Let the bees talk to each other – see how they get on. Ask them how they are going to help you with (*insert changes wanted*).

Now that all the bees know what they are doing and everyone is happy – watch the bees do the waggle dance. You might like to join in.

Note

1 Parts therapy was developed by Charles Tebbetts from the work of Paul Federn. Tebbetts' student Roy Hunter further developed the theory and his book *Hypnosis for Inner Conflict Resolution: Introducing Parts Therapy* (2005) is a very useful text.

Chapter 24

Butterflies passing by

Introduction

Over the years I have worked with many children who have experienced some form of loss – whether it be a person, a part of their own body or a sense of losing their childhood (perhaps due to being abused and never having had the opportunity to experience what is deemed to be a 'normal' childhood). The following script focuses on dealing with bereavement. A child can understand the concept of death from the age of six, and like an adult can sometimes need some support through the grieving process.

In recent years a growing concern of mine has been how many children have to deal with the aftermath of a suicide. I have become more aware of this through working in schools and colleges. I have worked with children whose parent has committed suicide and the child feels it has been their fault in some way. I have also worked with children who have experienced a fellow student killing themselves. In the latter circumstance, it can be useful to run group hypnotherapy sessions to say 'goodbye' and deal with unresolved issues.

Whatever the circumstances it is important that a child is supported and has the opportunity to vent their emotions and say 'goodbye'. A child can feel 'cheated' and 'guilty' because the death has been sudden and unexpected (especially in relation to a suicide) and consequently they never had the opportunity to say certain things or ask particular questions (perhaps about their family or heritage).

It can be hard for children (younger ones in particular) to understand why the death has occurred and they may have many questions. Everyone handles bereavement in their own way. A child may be surrounded by adults who are not talking about the person or their death; therefore, the child feels they cannot discuss it either. Sometimes a child struggles to verbalise their feelings about death so might feel more comfortable discussing emotions and asking the awkward questions whilst in trance.

It is really important that the hypnotherapist leaves plenty of time to work with this script. The child may have a lot to ask or say to the person who has passed. The session should never be rushed or cut short. So good preparation and planning are crucial for this type of bereavement work to be effective.

After the main script I have included two additional scripts which the hypnotherapist might like to use. A child can experience 'anniversary blues' and not know why they are feeling sad, but the subconscious mind is acknowledging the memory of a loss. Children often make contact with me saying they feel they need to come back but they don't know why, but I usually realise it is the time around they lost someone.

It can be beneficial to work with a child to help them work out a way of commemorating and remembering the person they have lost. They cannot always do this with people close to them – for fear of upsetting them. This was one of the reasons for including the letter written by Rex the rat to his deceased parents. Rex did not want to upset his grandma who was bringing him up after the death of both parents.

Writing things down can sometimes be more therapeutic than verbalising them. I have included Rex's letter because it can be read to a child in trance to illustrate that it is another way to express any sort of feeling that is difficult and to voice any fears for the future. A bereaved child can experience a whole gamut of emotions depending on the type of loss e.g. anger; sadness; guilt; deprivation. Once the letter has been read, work can be undertaken with the child to write their own letter if this is thought to be appropriate.

After undertaking bereavement work in trance, it is vital that the hypnotherapist finishes with a positive experience. Hopefully, the child will be feeling more positive due to the therapy but before bringing the child out of trance it can be good to do some simple relaxation work, either by taking the child to their safe place or using a relaxation script.

The script

In the summer months it is always possible to see large numbers of white butterflies flying around. Some fly alone – others fly together in groups, which make a beautiful picture. Butterflies are a bit like humans. There are times in life when a person wants and needs to be alone; at other times that same person might need to be with other people for support and comfort. Now I know you have experienced (*insert loss the child has experienced*) and there may be times when you want to talk about it and times when you don't.

Some people think that butterflies are passing souls. They are moving from their earth life to wherever they are going next. While they are deciding where they are going to go next, they are experiencing life as a butterfly. So while they are in this in-between stage they can move backwards and forwards in time and place; that is why some people sense a loved one who has passed is with them when they see a butterfly.

So I wonder if you might like to imagine that you are flying with a group of white butterflies. Imagine that you are up in the air flying over roads, houses, gardens, parks, fields – anywhere you want to go. You may be able to hear some sounds – coming from people, animals, traffic on the ground or aeroplanes up in the air. Wherever you are it is summertime, and the sun is out – shining brightly in the wonderful blue sky.

As you are enjoying flying with the beautiful white butterflies – feeling light and free – maybe you would like to start thinking about (*name of person who has died*) and wondering where s/he is now. Once someone has left this earth, they will leave behind part of themselves in our hearts and in the memories we have of them. Their energy and spirit will always be around you somewhere. So keep flying with the butterflies and think about the good times you had with (*name*). Relive some of those precious moments now and tell me about them.

(Guidance note: the hypnotherapist should encourage the child to talk about the memories and leave plenty of time to do so)

Maybe you feel sad that you did not get the chance to say some things you meant to say to (*name*). You may also have some questions you want to ask him/her. So let the butterflies take you higher and higher into the sky. Passing through any clouds that may be there – going higher and higher – up and up. You know you are flying up to meet (*name*).

I don't know what (*name*) will look like now – whether s/he will be in human form or something else, but you'll see him/her standing at some gates. Keep flying and tell me when you see him/her (*wait and then get a description of how the person is presenting*)

Now that (*name*) is here you can talk together. Do you want to stay here to do this or would you prefer to go somewhere else? Perhaps somewhere where you and (*name*) had good times together.

This is the time for you to:

(Guidance note: the hypnotherapist should guide the child through the following when/if appropriate)

- Say how you are feeling now
- Say how you have been feeling before today/past few days/weeks
- Say anything you need to say/meant to say to (*name*) but did not get the chance
- Ask any questions
- Discuss anything else that is important to you
- Relive any special memories
- Find out if (*name*) has anything to say to you
- Talk about anything that is bothering/worrying/frightening you.

So it is time to say 'goodbye' for now. (*Name*) will always be with you in your mind and in your heart. Let (*name*) go now and as s/he walks away you feel a sense of letting go but also a sense of peace.

So now it is time to fly again with the white butterflies; anytime you see a butterfly in the future you will recall pleasant memories of you and (*name*).

(Guidance note: if the hypnotherapist wishes the following additional scripts can be used)

Additional script 1: Remembering and commemorating

Your special mind can sometimes remember things when you are asleep – things that you don't remember when you are wide awake. So you might wake up one morning feeling a certain way and you don't know why. Perhaps you wake up one morning feeling very sad and you don't know why. It can be that it is a special date – a special day for you to remember someone. It could be the day someone died and this is why you feel sad. Your special mind remembers and when you remember, you might want to do something special to honour that person. To celebrate who they were, what they did – to have good thoughts about them.

I know you lost (*name*). How might you like to remember them? Would you like to do anything special – visit a special place; light a candle; release a balloon or something else? What would you like to do?

Additional Script 2: Rex the rat's letter to his mum and dad

I want to read to you the letter that Rex the rat wrote to his mum and dad, who had died when he was a baby rat. Rex needed to tell someone about how he felt.

Dear Mum and Dad,

> I feel terrible that I can't remember anything about you. You died when I was a baby rat. A terrible accident on the river; you were hit by a boat the day of the regatta. Grandma has shown me the place where the boat hit the riverbank and you died. I like to go there sometimes. It feels special and somewhere I feel close to you both. I'm going to bury this letter there a bit later when it gets very dark.
>
> Grandma looks after me very well and I love her to bits, but it's not the same as having living parents like the other rats have. I feel cheated that I have never had a proper family and that you have never been around to teach me things. Grandma has done everything you would have done but it's still not the same. I feel guilty saying this when Grandma is such a good and kind person.
>
> I feel very angry sometimes too. It doesn't seem fair that you both died at the same time. When I get angry, I chase humans to frighten them. I always feel bad later on when I think about what I have done. I don't really want to scare humans.
>
> I worry a lot too that someone else might die – like Grandma. Then what would I do? Grandma says I worry too much about everything and I spend too much time dwelling on things rather than getting on with life and enjoying it. I hate it when people say: "You should have moved on by now". Moved on to where?
>
> Yes, I do worry far too much – I know that – and I feel scared a lot of the time. I thought I'd write you this letter because I don't want to say this to anyone else – especially Grandma; I don't want to be a nuisance or for anyone to worry about me. Grandma would be very hurt if she knew I'd written this.
>
> So I'll finish off now and will bury this letter in that special place.
>
> Your loving son,
>
> Rex

So perhaps you might like to think about writing a letter to (*name*) now.

(Guidance note: the hypnotherapist can then encourage the child to write their own letter. The letter can be written whilst the child remains in trance or if the hypnotherapist prefers s/he can be brought back to the conscious state to do this)

Chapter 25

Lily Lavender's Wellbeing Shop

Introduction

The whole theme of the book is to promote a child's wellbeing and Lily Lavender's Wellbeing Shop will contribute very well to this. The script will be particularly helpful to children who have a hard time learning at school or who have had a teacher who is not very supportive with their learning needs. I wrote the script initially for children with dyslexia, who felt they would never succeed. Lily Lavender is a great role model for children of all ages. She demonstrates that a child can overcome obstacles with motivation and determination.

After the main script I have included four additional scripts which the hypnotherapist can use as required. They focus on: building confidence; getting rid of something; relaxation; promoting wellbeing. I have also included two appendices – Lily's wellbeing assessment and form – which can be used when a child is in or out of trance. If the hypnotherapist is going to be seeing the child on a regular basis then it is a tool which can be used at the beginning of each session to review and grade the child's wellbeing.

The script

We all know that people can be different and life would be very boring if we were all the same. We have to respect everyone as an individual – each human being is very special in the way they think, how they feel and how they behave. We are all good at something.

You probably know that you have five senses: sight, hearing, smell, taste and touch. Some of your senses may be stronger than others. Now I don't know about you but I love to smell nice things and I know a shop which is run by a woman called Lily Lavender. Lily had always liked nice smelly things ever since being a little girl. She used to spray her mum's perfumes all over herself, and often got told off when the perfume ran out very quickly. Lily had been determined from a very young age that one day she would have her own shop and sell all the lovely smelling things she liked as a child – like perfumes, soaps, shampoos and bubble bath.

Lily found lessons at school hard. She tried her best but it took her a long time to learn things; like spelling her name even though it was only short. She often used to write the letters of words the wrong way round. Some of the other children called her 'slow' or 'stupid'. When she went to the big school they found out she had something called dyslexia, which means it made it difficult for Lily to learn things. So Lily had problems with her reading, writing and spelling but she was determined she was not going to let this hold her back and she worked really hard all through school.

Lily loved science, particularly chemistry because she liked doing experiments and mixing things up. She was also very interested in what people sometimes refer to as alternative therapies. Lily liked things that were done in a different way – out of the ordinary – because she learnt to do things in her own special way. Teachers used to say Lily was a daydreamer because she often seemed to be far away in her thoughts. She was concentrating though – but in her own special way.

When she left school Lily trained to be a beautician and at the same time she became more and more interested in aromatherapy, which is sometimes known as essential oil therapy. To put it simply, oils which are taken from plants can help the mind, body and spirit. A bit like how hypnosis helps *you* to relax and (*insert problem being dealt with*).

From a very young age Lily had always been determined to run her own shop. For many years she *imagined* what it would be like to run her own shop. She *believed* she could do it and then she did *achieve* exactly what she wanted – she had her own shop which sold lovely smelling things. Lily used to say to herself everyday: '*Imagine – Believe – Achieve.*'

I think you might enjoy visiting Lily's shop. Just let your mind drift as I tell you a bit about Lily's shop so you can imagine what it is like.

Lily's shop is to be found down a little, narrow cobbled street. So just imagine you are walking down this quiet cobbled street. There are several doors on both the right and the left. Some doors lead into shops, others into offices and some are people's houses. Now just keep walking down the street until you see the sign outside a shop which says 'Lily Lavender's Wellbeing Shop'. Can you see it? What does the sign look like?

Have a look in the shop window. What do you see?

Now go in the door. You find yourself in a big room. Take a deep breath – can you smell anything?

There is a shop counter somewhere in this room and shelves on every wall. The shelves are covered with lots of things: bottles of all shapes and sizes; candles – all different colours; burners; glass jars; thin little sticks; soaps; brushes; combs and sponges. Can you see anything else?

Just go and explore. Look at all these lovely things. Pick up anything you like and have a look. Maybe pick up a bottle and feel how heavy or light it is. What is the bottle made of? What colour is it? Is there a label on the bottle? (*if so, what does it say?*)

There are probably some tester bottles about so you can smell some oils or fragrances.

Now behind the counter there is another door. There is a sign on the door saying 'Wellbeing Room'. This is where some of Lily's customers come for their treatments; it is a place where people can relax and feel better. Lily is a trained beautician so some customers ask her to make their nails look nice or to shape their eyebrows; others like to have a face massage. Lily also uses some of the products from her shop to help her customers deal with a problem and make them feel better. I think some of Lily's products and treatments might be able to help you.

(Guidance note: at this point the hypnotherapist can decide whether to use one of the additional scripts below)

Additional script 1: The relaxing candle wax

Lily Lavender has lots of candles in her shop. All different shapes and sizes and smells. Go to where are all the candles are displayed in the shop and choose one. Now this candle can help you to concentrate very well and then relax very deeply.

Imagine that you are looking at the candle and that it is burning. Look at the flame flickering. Look deep into the flame. You see different colours in the flame – yellow; orange; red; blue and purple. Now if you look towards the bottom of the flame you might see a tiny bit of black – that is the wick of the candle.

It is very relaxing just watching the flame flickering, but as you watch it more and more you come to realise that at the bottom of the little bit of blackness there is a pool of liquid. The flame is melting the top of the candle making a pool of liquid around the wick of the candle.

You will feel a gentle warmth coming from the flame. I wonder if you can smell anything from the candle as it continues to burn.

Look deep into that pool of liquid. You see the melted wax is moving towards to the candle's edge. The liquid is moving slowly and gently as the candle continues to burn and the flame continues to flicker.

The liquid is reaching the edge of the candle and is about to run over the edge. Watch it carefully now as it starts moving down and down the outside of the candle. Slowly and gently on its journey – down and down the candle.

As you follow the liquid moving down and down you feel calmer and calmer. You feel relaxed – not a care in the world. Your eyelids may be feeling heavy – in a good way. They are becoming heavier and heavier. It is so good for you to take some time out to just relax. Don't think about anything – just feel the calmness and relaxation.

Keep watching the liquid as it goes down and down. I wonder if it is changing in any way as it goes on its journey. Maybe the liquid is turning slowly into a soft wax. It is nearly halfway down the candle now. You are feeling even calmer – more relaxed.

Continue to watch the liquid on its journey. Still travelling down and down – so very gently and slowly – but also changing very slowly into a soft wax.

The liquid wax is now near the very bottom of the candle – nearly there – and as it reaches the bottom you feel completely relaxed and at peace with yourself.

Additional script 2: Wash it away

Lily has lots of things in her shop that can wash things away or just make you feel better on the outside and inside.

Is there something you would like to wash away? – a thought, a feeling or behaviour (*or insert anything else the child has already discussed*).

Have another look around Lily's shop. See what you can find to wash away (*what the child has said*). I know Lily has soaps, hand and body washes, shower gels, face scrubs and lots of other things. Choose whatever you like and tell me what it is.

Lily likes her customers to test things out before they buy anything. There is a washbasin in the corner of the shop with a small hand towel at the side. Go over and turn the taps on. Put a bit of (*what the child has chosen*) into the palm of your hands and rub it in. Put a little bit of water into your hands. Watch as the water makes your hands full of foam and bubbles.

Think about what you are going to wash away. Wash your hands really well. When you are ready rinse your hands under the taps. Keep rinsing your hands. Watch the foam and bubbles go down the plughole – feel (*whatever the child is washing away*) leaving you. Listen for the gurgles as it all goes down the drain and is washed away. Tell me when it's gone completely.

Now dry your hands on the towel and let's make sure everything is going to be smooth for the future. So look around again and find some lotion, cream or moisturiser. They'll be in tubes and bottles; all different colours and lovely smells. Lily won't mind if you test a few out to make sure you get the right one for you. So go ahead – find the right one. Tell me when you have it and what you have chosen.

Smooth (*what the child has chosen*) into your hands. Maybe put some on your face, arms and legs. Just feel the (*what the child has chosen*) going into the pores of your skin – making your skin feel smooth. So everything in the future will be perfectly smooth.

Go and find Lily now and tell her which products you would like to take home with you and she will wrap them up for you. You will be able to use these products any time when you need to wash away something or you need to smooth things out.

Additional script 3: Bottle of confidence (*or motivation, determination or something else relevant for the child*)

Now you have told me that you have some difficulty with (*lack of confidence*). Just go to the shelf where you can see lots of different coloured bottles and they all have labels on them. Have a good look through and find a bottle that you really like. Take the bottle in your hand and pull the stopper out. Just take a deep breath in and smell; then imagine the smell going into the nostrils in your nose and starting its journey into your head and then around your body. Breathe in (*confidence*) slowly and deeply; feel the (*confidence*) grow as it moves inside you – getting stronger and stronger. It reaches every part of you inside – from the very top of you – your head. To the very bottom of you – the tips of your toes. Breathe in from the bottle again. Feeling even more confident now. That is fantastic.

Now just take another deep breath and smell again. Breathing in (*confidence*) slowly and deeply; feeling the (*confidence*) continuing to grow as it moves inside you – getting stronger and stronger. Feeling more and more confident.

There is a label on the bottle and the word 'Confidence' is written on it. I want you to put this Bottle of Confidence somewhere safe where you can reach it easily – like in a pocket or up a sleeve. Put it somewhere now and then tap it twice wherever you have put it. If in the future you need a boost of confidence, just tap your bottle twice and you will feel the confidence growing stronger and stronger inside you.

Additional script 4: Lily Lavender's wellbeing assessment

Lily Lavender sells lots of things in her shop which will help people with their physical health and also their mental health. Both types of health are important and it is a good idea to look after them – not wait until something goes wrong.

Lily has a lot of people coming into her shop. Some customers come in to buy nice things as a treat for themselves; others want to buy a present for someone else. Sadly, some people come in because they have a problem. Lily is always there to help in any way she can. Lily believes very strongly that it is important to talk about things, not keep them bottled up inside; and if someone finds it difficult or painful to talk then she finds another way of getting the information out in the open without making them feel uncomfortable.

Lily believes that wellbeing is a very important thing in life, but what is wellbeing? It means different things to different people and this is what Lily likes to find out. So she has designed her own special way of doing it.

Lily invites people who have a problem into her Wellbeing Room. The room is very spacious but simple – no clutter. There is a bed if someone wants to lie down. There are two chairs if someone prefers to sit – one for the customer and one for Lily herself. There is a very small table with just a few things Lily uses regularly: paper, pens, and crayons.

So this is how Lily would get you to think about your wellbeing.

> Think back over the last week. Think about all the things you have done and the conversations you have had (prompt: *at home; school; college; other places; early morning; daytime; night-time*). Just take your time and remember all things you have said and done.
>
>   As you are going through your week, think about your feelings.
>   Think about what you enjoyed doing.
>   Think about things you did not enjoy.
>   So let's think about how you are feeling today. Let's do it by using numbers. 'Ten' means you are feeling really really good. 'One' would mean you are not feeling very good at all.
>   So tell me – between one and ten where are you today?
>   Thank you.
>   So I want to learn a little more about you. If that would be OK with you – then I would like to ask you some questions.
>   What makes you happy?
>   What makes you unhappy?
>   Is anything making you unhappy at the moment?
>   What could make things better?
>   What changes would you like to make?
>   So you said today you feel like a number (*insert*). What needs to happen to enable you to have a good week and increase that number?
>   What number would you like to be by next week (*or next session*)?
>   What do you need to do/change to achieve this?
>   What are your hopes for the future?

Appendix 1: How to do the assessment of wellbeing

How to use the form

The following form can be printed out by the hypnotherapist, then used to assess a child's wellbeing in the conscious state initially. This assessment of wellbeing is more detailed than the one presented above in additional script 4 which was developed for use in trance. This assessment can be adapted to suit the age of the child.

Question 1: first of all, the hypnotherapist gets the child to grade their wellbeing by just going with their gut.

Question 2: the aim is to get the child to list all the things they need in their life for their wellbeing to be good. With younger children different words should be used as they are unlikely to understand the term 'wellbeing'. I've used the word 'good' on the assessment form; the hypnotherapist may choose to use another word e.g. happy; content. The aim is to get the child to focus on both their physical and mental health.

The hypnotherapist should not lead the child but sometimes it is helpful to give some prompts to help the child think about a range of things. For example:

- People
- Relationships: family; friends; teachers; tutors; coaches
- Pets
- Possessions
- Home
- School
- Food/drink
- Interests
- Activities; hobbies; games; sports

For Question 2 there are 15 lines drawn on the form. The child may only have a few things listed initially. Older children may have many more.

Scoring: once the child has a list, each individual item is then scored using the one to ten scale again. The scores are then added up to get a *total score*, which is then divided by however many items there are in order to get the *average score* which becomes the wellbeing score.

Appendix 2: Assessment of wellbeing form

1. Just go with your gut – don't think about this too much. Let's think about how you are feeling today. Let's do it by using numbers. 'Ten' means you are feeling really really good. 'One' would mean you are not feeling very good at all. So tell me - between one and ten where are you today?

    Score [   ]

2. Make a list of things that you need in your life to make you feel good. Think about things you need every day/week.

                                                                                              SCORE

    - ....   [   ]

    - ....   [   ]

    - ....   [   ]

- .... [   ]
- .... [   ]
- .... [   ]
- .... [   ]
- .... [   ]
- .... [   ]
- .... [   ]
- .... [   ]
- .... [   ]
- .... [   ]
- .... [   ]
- .... [   ]

3. Total score: [   ]
4. Average score i.e. wellbeing [   ]
5. What score are you aiming for next week? [   ]
6. What do you need to change/work on to achieve this?

Chapter 26

The Fairy House

Introduction

This script was originally written for very young children, but a lot of people (including adults) seem to like fairies and all things magical so a hypnotherapist might decide to use it for older children.

The main objective is to work on specific issues using the magic wand and fairy dust as anchors, but of course other anchors can be created when using the script. It is a script which can be used to work on a wide variety of issues which relate particularly to thoughts and feelings.

The script can also be used to focus solely on promoting the child's wellbeing. Fairies are very health conscious so the hypnotherapist can use the fairies to get the child thinking about healthy eating, growing things (in the physical or emotional sense).

The script

I would like to tell you about the Fairy House, which is a very magical place. If you walked past it you might not realise that it is a Fairy House. It stands right opposite a cinema on an odd piece of land, set back from the road and a grass verge. It is surrounded by trees and on the ground all around it there are small cobblestones. Around the edge of the cobblestones there are small pathways made of grass leading to the long grass verge which runs alongside the road. People tend to walk right past the Fairy House without noticing it all because they are so eager to get to the cinema.

I do not know how much you know about fairies, but I can tell you they are very kind beings who are there to help. We all need a bit of help sometimes. Fairies like to see things grow. They particularly like plants, flowers and trees, and they also think it is important for children to grow in strength and confidence (*insert anything else the child needs to work on*).

Fairies are also very good at healing, making things better, and they are especially good at protecting people and things. They don't like things to get broken.

Fairies have magical powers but they also have things to help them like wands and fairy dust. They need to keep up their strength because they work very hard, so they eat well and at regular intervals. They particularly like to drink lots of milk and eat anything with honey in it – especially honey cakes. There are beehives in the fairy garden at the back of the house, so the fairies are never short of honey, which is so good for them.

The Fairy House looks quite small from the outside. It looks like a turret that has been taken off a castle and placed on the ground. It is made of big stones and has a pointed steeple pointing up to the sky. There is a wooden door on the front of the Fairy House with a large iron knocker on it. To get the fairies' attention, you have to knock on the door very hard three times and shout: 'Hello Fairies. I want to come in please'. Why don't you give it a try now? Knock three times. If the fairies are not too busy and have time to help, the door will open. Oh look – the door is opening very slowly – in you go.

As you go into the Fairy House, it is very dark but you see sparkles flashing within the darkness. There are all different coloured sparkles. Follow the sparkles. Try to guess where they will appear next. Now go further into house and shout 'Hello Fairies'. Wait for the fairies to appear. Be patient though – they might not appear immediately.

Fairies can help with all sorts of problems but you have to tell them exactly what is the matter. So I am sure someone will be along very shortly to speak with you. When a fairy does appear, the Fairy House will become very bright and at the same time you may experience a lightness inside of you. Just tell me when you see the fairy who has come to help you.

Look at the fairy and thank her for coming to meet you. Look at her beautiful dress and wings, and notice that she is carrying a magic wand. This wand is very special because it can get rid of many things which are not helpful to a person (*insert examples of feelings, emotions, pain, but include an issue the child has told you about*).

This fairy is here to help you. She knows a lot about you already because she knew you would be paying a visit to the Fairy House one day and has been watching you in the day when you are at home, school, other places and also at night when you are fast asleep. She knows the best way to help you and will always be there for you in the future if you need her. So just have a chat with her now about what has been troubling you (*mention issue then leave some time for the child to talk to the fairy*). Tell me when you have finished chatting with the fairy.

Good – now follow the fairy; she is going to take you into a room where the fairies make the magic wands and lots of other magical things. When you go into the room you see lots and lots of fairies being very busy. The fairy goes towards a row of cupboards on the wall and opens one. She brings out a wand and says: 'We have made this one for you. It is very good in whooshing things away. Making them disappear quickly and forever'.

Another fairy then comes along to speak to you and she has a little cloth bag in her hand. She opens the bag and shows you inside. She explains to you:

> This is fairy dust, which has magical powers. You can sprinkle it on yourself to make you feel better or feel a certain way. Or you can sprinkle it on things to make them disappear. It could be fun to get rid of (*insert something which has been discussed e.g. a feeling, thought, behaviour*).

> Another thing you might like to try – the fairy dust can help you to fly like fairies do – if you would like to do that – you can go wherever want to go. Maybe to get away from things – take some time out.

Fairy dust can also help things to grow (*insert something relevant to the child e.g. confidence; courage to ask a question/say something*).

It can mend or heal things (*insert something relevant to the child e.g. emotions – sadness, upset, loss – perhaps due to a bereavement; parents separating/divorcing*).

One of the best things is fairy dust can create anything – it can make your wishes come true (*insert something relevant to the child e.g. a place to feel safe*).

It is very kind of the fairies to give you the wand and fairy dust. Would you like to go out into the fairy garden now and play with the wand and fairy dust? You can ask the fairies to come with you if you like.
(Guidance note: the hypnotherapist can then work with the child on relevant issues using the wand and/or fairy dust)

Chapter 27

Getting rid of stuff at the business centre

Introduction

This is another script that can be used to get rid of something. My therapy room is in a business centre and many children who have come for therapy have found things of interest inside and outside the building. So this script lends itself to disposal of anything – the common theme being a thought, feeling or behaviour but specifically it could be a memory of something bad happening: a specific fear, phobia or habit.

The script

You know already that your thoughts, feelings and behaviours are all connected, and sometimes you need to change the way you think and feel to help you behave in a different way. Sometimes you need to get rid of stuff by throwing it away and that stuff could be a thought, feeling or behaviour. So maybe you would like to think about something that you would like to get rid of (*insert a particular issue if appropriate*). Make yourself comfortable and start thinking about that. While you are thinking about (*whatever is to be thrown away*) I want to tell you about a business centre, where there are many offices in which people work at different jobs and because it has so many good places and equipment to get rid of stuff.

The business centre is located right next to the river. I want you to imagine that you are sitting by the side of the river. It is a beautiful warm, sunny day and you are feeling very relaxed. Imagine there is a chair in front of you. In a moment when I count to 3, whatever you want to get rid of (*or insert what has already been identified*) will appear on that chair. I have no idea what it will look like. Are you ready? 1, 2, and 3.

What do you see on the chair? (*get a full description and remember it could be an object, person or animal*).

Is there anything you want to say to (X) before you get rid of it?
(*Guidance note: the hypnotherapist should encourage the child to speak to X i.e. say anything they need to say; talk about how they feel. Throughout this conversation the hypnotherapist should check how X reacts i.e. enquire whether X says anything; how does X look?*)

Next you need to find a box or something else to put (X) in.
(*Guidance note: you might need to suggest the child shrink the thing if it is something big*)

Good. Now pack (X) into the box and put a lid on it and seal it up if you want to – maybe find some glue or Sellotape.

So when you are ready, pick up the box. How heavy does it feel? Carry the box and walk away from the river. The business centre is not very far away – a short walk. Go and see if you can find a way into the business centre and tell me when you get there. Good. You might like to put the box down while you look round the business centre. That's right.

Lots of different businesses and people work in the offices in the business centre. The offices are all different shapes and sizes. Some people work alone in a small office; the big offices may have lots of people in them. Can you see into the offices? Can you see anyone? What are they doing? Is anyone walking about outside?

You might even see some birds and animals too as the business centre looks onto the river. Rex the rat has been known to pay a visit now and again and frighten some of the office workers! He is harmless, but many people don't like his long tail. Birds, bees and butterflies fly all around the business centre. Many workers get distracted from what they are doing as they start looking out of the window – they start to daydream.

There is a large car park at the front of business centre and in the car park there are six huge bins where people put all the rubbish and waste from their offices. So many things are put in these bins – paper – cardboard boxes – food – empty bottles and cans – and sometimes the strangest things you'd never expect to find there. Open the bins and have a look in – what can you see?

There are other good places and things to help to get rid of stuff here in the business centre:

- Some offices have paper shredders
- In the kitchen there is a waste disposal unit
- There are so many plug holes – in the kitchen, toilets and the shower room. So lots of things can be washed away.
- The caretaker, Malik, has to keep the business centre in a state of good repair. The landlord employs Malik to keep the business centre looking good but it also has to be very efficient. So Malik keeps a lot of tools locked away in his equipment room.

Can you find anything else that you think might be helpful to get rid of stuff?

So you want to get rid of the box you bought with you to the business centre, don't you? You've seen lots of places where you could get rid of it. Where would you like to do this? How are you going to do it exactly?

OK – so go and collect the box and get rid of it and its contents (*encourage the child to describe how they are disposing of the box*). How good does that feel? (*encourage the child to describe how they are feeling as they dispose of the box*).

(*Guidance note: the hypnotherapist works with the child to dispose of the box Whilst doing this emphasising the feelings of release. After this has been done the hypnotherapist might like to embed any commands they think will be beneficial*)

You can come back to the business centre anytime you need to get rid of any other stuff for good.

Chapter 28

The post office

Introduction

I developed the main script initially for very young children who had been abused, with the objective that they could enjoy the idea of playing in a post office but at the same time could talk about things that were difficult. I later adapted it for use with older children and developed further scripts.

The main script presented below introduces the child to the post office and then the four additional scripts can be used to undertake the more in-depth work. The hypnotherapist can choose to use just one additional script or some can be combined together.

All the scripts offer the opportunity for children to express themselves in different ways and really help a child who finds it hard to talk verbally by offering alternative ways of 'talking' (i.e. drawing, painting, writing). It is hoped that a child will continue to use some of the methods introduced when they are in the conscious state.

The scripts can help children get rid of anything that is hindering them e.g. a memory of what has happened; a feeling or a fear. Whatever method the child has used to express him/herself – producing a picture, writing a letter – if they need to get rid of it, the additional script 'Posting a Parcel' can be used to finally get rid of it.

I have used these scripts for abused children but also for children who have been bereaved and cannot say things face-to-face to the living or they want to say things to the person who has passed.

The fourth additional script is about protection and promoting a feeling of safety. This script works well for children who have a fear or phobia but is particularly effective for children who are being bullied.

The script

A post office is a very important place; it can be located in the centre of a community and a place where people bump into each other and have a chat. It can provide many essential services, which are useful to all sorts of people. A major role it has is to send things away – as far as they need to go. I think it might be helpful for you to imagine a very special post office, so that you could get rid of some things that you do not need. You can send anything you want anywhere – as far away as you like.

So just close your eyes and let yourself get comfortable. Breathing slowly and gently as you know how to do. Feeling nice and relaxed and ready to find the special post office.

Imagine that you are walking along a street. Take your time and just enjoy your walk – looking on either side of you and in front – going forwards, always going forwards. Just keep walking until you find the special post office. You'll know when you have nearly got there because you will see a red post box on the pavement. Tell me when you find it.

This particular post office is special because it has all sorts of helpful things inside it. So when you are ready open the door and go into the post office. There will be a counter somewhere and lots of shelves all around with important things on them.

So go and have a look at the counter first. Can you see someone behind it? That person is there to help you – you only have to ask.

Now go and have a look at the shelves and see if you can find some of these things: boxes; brown paper for wrapping parcels; different kinds of paper for wrapping presents; string; bubble wrap; Sellotape; envelopes; padded envelopes; cards; postcards; writing paper; pens; pencils; crayons; glue – I wonder what else you can find.
(Guidance note: at this point the hypnotherapist can choose to use one of the following alternatives)

Additional script 1: Draw or paint a picture

It can be difficult to talk about certain things when we have been hurt in some way. We might not like what someone has said or done to us or the way someone has made us feel. We may have been told not to tell anybody. For whatever reason a person finds it difficult to talk about something that has happened, it can be good to tell the story using something other than your voice.

Children who find it hard to speak – or to find the right words – can find it easier to draw or paint a picture that can tell their story in a picture.

Maybe you would like to draw or paint something whilst you are in this post office. What would you like to do? See what you can find on the shelves to help you draw/paint *(prompt if needed: pens, pencils, crayons, paints, paper, card)*.

In the corner of the post office you'll see a chair and table. You can draw/paint your picture there. Go and settle yourself down.
(Guidance note: the hypnotherapist works with the child as they imagine drawing or painting the picture whilst in trance. It is important not to rush the child but the following questions can be used as prompts if appropriate)

Tell me about the picture.
What are you drawing/painting?
Who/what is in the picture?
What does the picture show?
When you look at the picture how does it make you feel?
Do you need to change anything in the picture?
Do you need to add anything to the picture?

Now that you have drawn/painted that picture – where would you like it to go? How are you going to send it from the special post office? You can send it any way you like – by post, special delivery or by a courier. You will need to wrap it up first – so do that now.

Are you ready to send it away? How are you going to do this? The person behind the counter can help you. Do it now – send the picture away. See it go. How do you feel now?

Additional script 2: Writing a letter

When you cannot say something to someone's face, it can sometimes make you feel better if you write what you want to say in a letter. Would you like to write a letter? Who do you want to write the letter to?

So why don't you go and find some writing paper that you like and a pen (*wait – then ask the child to describe what they have chosen*). In the corner of the post office you'll see a chair and table. Take your paper and pen; go and settle yourself down.

Just sit for as long as you like and think about what you want to say. When you feel the time is right, begin to write your letter.

(Guidance note: the hypnotherapist works with the child as s/he is writing the letter. It is imperative that the hypnotherapist encourages the child to take their time writing the letter especially when they may be finding some parts difficult to write.

Throughout, the hypnotherapist should be talking about the feelings of letting go/ release. The following questions can be used as prompts if required)

Tell me what you are writing about in the letter.
What are you thinking about as you are writing the letter?
How are you feeling as you are writing the letter?
Perhaps you would like to read a sentence/paragraph to me?
How does that make you feel when you read the words out loud?
Does it make you want to change any words?
Do want to say anything else?
Do you need to say anything else but are finding it hard to find the right words?
Have you put everything in the letter that you want to?
Now read the letter from start to finish.
Do you need to change or add anything?
How do you feel now?
Well done – you have written a really good letter. Now you need to find an envelope to put it in – do that now (*wait…then ask the child to describe the envelope they have chosen*). So you are nearly finished now – would you like to put your letter in the envelope and then seal it? You just need to get a stamp now from the person behind the counter.

Now I want you to continue breathing nice and slowly, then when you are ready take a really deep breath and look through the post office window to where the red post box is standing on the pavement. When you are ready – leave the post office and go and post your letter.

How do you feel now?

Additional script 3: Posting a parcel

A post office has so many things that can help you send away anything which is not helpful to you or is making you unhappy (*or any other negative emotion the child has discussed*). You have been telling me about (*insert issue*). I wonder if you would like to post that off somewhere and get rid of it for good. Have another look around the shelves and then tell me how you are going to pack up (*issue*), make a parcel and put it in the post.

(Guidance note: the hypnotherapist works with the child to pack up the parcel. It is important for the hypnotherapist to talk to the child about what they are feeling as they are packing up, but also emphasising the positive feelings of release)

You have made a really good job of packing up (*issue*). Now you need to go to the counter and ask the person behind it to weigh it for you. Goodness, it is very heavy. It must have been weighing you down for some time. It will be good to post it off and get rid of it completely, but to do that you need some stamps. So ask the person behind the counter to help you find the right stamps and put them on the parcel.

Finally, it is all good to go. When you are ready, hand over the parcel to the person behind the counter, who will put it in one of the big sacks you can see. That's right – in it goes. Oh look who has just come through the door – the postman who collects the sacks and other things to take away. Watch him as he has a chat with the person behind the counter before s/he lets him in behind the counter to collect the sacks.

Watch carefully now as the postman picks up the sack with your parcel in it. Watch him go through the door and put the sacks into his van. Feel that sense of leaving and of letting go. As you watch the van drive off say a final 'goodbye' to (*the issue*) – it has gone forever. Never to be seen (*or felt*) again.

Additional script 4: Invisible bubble wrap

The post office sells big rolls of bubble wrap, so that people can wrap up things that are precious and which they do not want to get broken in the post. The bubble wrap can protect all sorts of things. Bubble wrap has other uses as well. It gives you such a lovely feeling just to pop those little bubbles and listen to the sound they make. You can have such fun doing that – would you like to have a go now? Go to the shelves and take down one of the big rolls of bubble wrap.

(Guidance note: let the child pop the bubble wrap. This can be for relaxation and fun, but it can also be used to release any tension. It is up to the hypnotherapist how they want to work this)

The roll of bubble wrap you have picked out is actually very special – it has magical powers to protect you. It does this by becoming invisible to everyone else – except you. You will know that it is always there – protecting you all the time. This could be really useful when you are feeling (*insert any negative feeling discussed*).

Just look at the huge roll of bubble wrap now. Imagine that you are starting to unroll it and then start wrapping it all around your body. Start at your feet; wrap them up. Then keep going – wrap up your legs – both of them. You are starting to feel very safe. Then wrap up the middle of your body – round and round the bubble wrap goes – feeling safe and protected – nothing can hurt you inside or out. You better do your head next and leave your arms to last. Round and round the bubble wrap goes – not too tight – just right. There is plenty of room to keep breathing very naturally. Now the bubble wrap with its magical powers will help you to wrap up your arms – feeling even safer now – more protected.

Be aware of how safe you feel inside your bubble wrap. Nothing can get past the bubble wrap; it is always there to protect you and keep you safe. It will never ever go away. All you have to do now is make it invisible to everyone else. You will always be able to imagine the bubble wrap around you. You know and will remember that the bubble wrap is around all of you – doing its job of making you feel safe and protected. So tell the bubble wrap to become invisible – do that now. Fantastic. You know the bubble wrap is still there and it will make you feel safe anytime you feel (*insert feeling discussed or any other situation as appropriate*).

Chapter 29

The art gallery

Introduction

I have used the art gallery in all sorts of different ways but essentially its main purpose is to work on issues regarding negative self-image, lack of self-belief, and the long-term effects of bullying in order to promote a child's wellbeing. There is such an emphasis on image nowadays and a child can be badly affected by what people say about how they look or present themselves. Comments and actions from others can have devastating long-term effects. Therefore, this script can be very powerful when working with children who have been bullied or abused.

The script can also help those who may be experiencing some difficulties around their sexuality or gender identity, or who have developed eating problems. However, I would say that working with eating disorders is a specialist area and I would advise newly qualified hypnotherapists in particular to undertake some specialist training as part of their Continued Professional Development (CPD) if they want to practise in this area.

The script initially tells the story of Leah and Malik, two artists who struggled with different issues in their childhoods and early adulthoods, but eventually achieved their ambitions. Therefore, the central theme is about not giving up but having determination. I have included three additional scripts, which can be used to address how the child views him/herself; to work on self-esteem and to believe in themselves (rather than believing what others have told them in the past).

The script

Leah and Malik have an art gallery – but it is not your typical art gallery with paintings hanging on the walls. It does exhibit art works but it also has lots of large and small spaces so events and activities can take place. Leah and Malik want to help people in the community using art. Let me tell you a little bit about Leah and Malik: neither of them has had easy lives.

Leah has had problems with food and eating from a very early age. She was never happy living with her family; her mum and dad were always fighting. Since being born Leah has always been underweight and very thin. When she was a teenager, she was diagnosed with an eating disorder. She was called all sorts of horrid names by other children at school because her bones stuck out. Leah hated getting changed for P.E. lessons and doing sports or any kind of exercise. What Leah was really good at was drawing, painting and making things. When she was thinking about applying to go to art college a very unhelpful art teacher told her: 'You think you're an artist but you're not good enough to be a successful one'. So Leah did not apply for art college.

Leah had lots of different jobs over the years but she always continued to paint. She often felt very sad because people still called her horrible names and made fun of her being so thin. Sometimes Leah felt really low and she would not go out of her house for days. After not doing much for days except crying and feeling that everything was pointless, she would eventually start to paint, which helped her to feel better. She was doing something she liked but she still did not think she was good enough to be a full-time artist.

Malik similarly had had problems at school. This was because he was partially deaf and people made fun of him. He could lip-read but sometimes got things a bit wrong. Malik got called horrible names because of his hearing problem but also because he was a Muslim. The way he dealt with it through his teenage years was to grow his hair a long way down his back – almost to his waist. He felt safe hiding under his hair and he wore very dark, baggy clothes. However, his hair and clothes just attracted more horrible comments from people who thought he was a 'weirdo'.

Malik also struggled because he knew he was attracted to other boys rather than girls, and did not feel he had anyone to talk to about this. When he eventually did tell his family, they rejected him and he had to leave home. Malik was really good at making sculptures and he continued to sculpt when he grew up.

Neither Leah nor Malik gave up what they loved doing but they both lacked belief and confidence in themselves. This was all due to all the horrible and hurtful things that had been said to them repeatedly over the years. When something negative is said a lot, you can start to believe it is true.

Leah and Malik first met when Leah did some temping work in one of the offices in a business centre. Malik worked as a part-time caretaker in the business centre. They both needed to do more than one job in order to keep up their painting and sculpting. Leah and Malik became good friends because they had a lot in common, both loving art. They eventually told each other a lot about their childhoods, the problems they had experienced with their families and at school.

Life changed for Leah when she applied to take part in a local exhibition. Artists were chosen and then sponsored by businesses to paint statues of owls, which were then located throughout the city. There were sixty owls in total placed around the city. Children and adults would walk through the city to find the owls – they called it the Owl Hunt. Leah's owl was put in front of the town hall. At the end of six months the owls were auctioned off to raise money for the local children's hospital. People loved Leah's owl and from then on she sold lots of her paintings and was asked to make lot of things.

Malik's life changed too around that time. He sold a sculpture to a man from America who was visiting the local area and who really liked Malik's work. He then commissioned more sculptures and word spread so Malik started getting requests from people in America for both big and small sculptures.

As their art work started to sell, Leah and Malik began thinking about packing in their part-time jobs. They decided to rent a building, where they could open an art gallery. They wanted to exhibit their own work but they also wanted to help other people in the community. Because of what they had been through themselves, they believed that art therapy could be very good for people. So they ran classes and events, but they also rented out rooms so people could just come and paint on their own or they could use the rooms that had different resources in them: paints, brushes, pens, crayons, pencils, canvases, paper, and frames.

Leah and Malik never gave up on their dreams of becoming full-time artists. They worked hard and eventually when their works started to sell, they started to believe in themselves and forgot all the horrible comments that had been said to them over the years.

Would you like to go to have a look inside Leah and Malik's art gallery and do some painting or craft work yourself?

(Guidance note: the hypnotherapist can choose how to proceed with the alternative scripts given below)

Additional script 1: Self-portrait

In the art gallery there are small rooms where people can come in and paint on their own. They know they won't be disturbed. They are very private and safe rooms. So imagine that you are standing outside a door to one of these rooms and on the count of three you will go in – *1, 2,* and *3*.

Take a look around. You will see some easels and different sized canvases. First choose a canvas that you would like to paint on and then find an easel to put it on. Then look around for some paintbrushes and some paints. You will find some thick oil paints but maybe you would prefer to use water-based paints. Choose whatever is right for you.

You are going to paint a self-portrait. You have told me that you are shy and you want to be more confident. Think about how you would like to be and how you might look.

(Guidance note: prompt the child to think about how they want to be. Some suggested prompts follow)

What changes do you want to make?
What would make you feel confident?

Now start to paint how the new confident you would look.

How would you hold your head?
Where would your eyes be looking?
How would you have your hair?
What would you wear?
How would you stand exactly?
Where would your arms be?
Your legs and feet?

Keep painting until you have completed the new confident you.

Additional script 2: An exhibition – The life of ...

Leah and Malik often organise short-term exhibitions and this month they have organised an exhibition of photographs telling the story of your life. They have invited you in today to see the exhibition before it opens tomorrow.

Imagine that you are in the art gallery and you are going to find the exhibition called 'The Life of (*insert child's name*)'

The photographs in the exhibition tell the story of your life – the good things and the bad. So take a deep breath and go into your exhibition. You see all the photographs on the walls have been framed. Now go and start looking at the photographs – they will bring back lots of memories – some good but maybe some that are not so good.

As you walk around tell me what you see.

(Guidance note: when the child sees a bad memory, the hypnotherapist should start working on changing the photograph)

Tell me about the photograph.
Who is in it?
What is happening?
How are you feeling in the photograph (*if the child is in it*)?
How are you feeling as you are looking at the photograph?
What would you like to do with this photograph?

(Guidance note: the child will either want to change what is happening in the photograph or take that particular photograph out of the exhibition completely)

If the child wants to makes changes
So you want to change what is happening in the photograph. What do you want to change exactly? How are you going to do it?
Do you want to take someone out? Put someone in? Change what someone is doing?
Do you want to change what you did?
Do you want to change what you said or how you said something?
Do you want to change the way you feel?
Are you sure you have made all the changes you want in the photograph?
Finally, do you want to change the frame of the photograph?
What is the current frame like? What is it made of? What colour is it?
What new frame would you like to put around the photograph?

If the child wants to take the photograph out of the exhibition
So you are going to throw out this photograph – that's fine. Do that now. Find somewhere to get rid of it for good.
How do you feel now the photograph has gone forever?
There is a space on the wall now. So you need to find a replacement photograph. Think back to a time when you were happy, having fun.
Who was there?
What were you doing?
How were you feeling?

Just keep remembering and enjoying that time. Now you need to capture it. Take a photograph of the best moment. Great – you've captured it and can treasure it.

Now get a printed copy of the photograph and hold it in front of you. You need to put a frame around it. What sort of frame are you going to put it in? OK – so go and find the frame. When it is ready, you can put the photograph on the wall. How good does that look?

So have one last look around your exhibition. Make sure everything is in the right place and just as you want it to be.

Additional script 3: Painting the walls

There is one big empty room in the art gallery where you can do anything you want with the things you find in the little room that runs off the big room. So when you are ready just go into the room and see how empty it is. Look at the four walls of the room – what colour are they?

Find the door to the little room which goes off the big room. Open it and see all the tins of paint that are in there – every colour you could ever imagine. You'll also find paintbrushes, turpentine; bleach; rags; dusters; rubber gloves; bin bags. Everything you need.

Now go and sit in the middle of the room. I know this might not be very pleasant to do but it won't last long. Just think of the times when someone has been nasty to you (*use specific examples if a child has disclosed certain incidents*). Think of the words, phrases or sentences that have been said to you. The word and phrases that have hurt you.

Go into the cupboard – choose a paintbrush and a tin of paint. What colour is the paint?

Think of those words, phrases or sentences and paint them on the walls in the room. As you paint each word, phrase or sentence tell me what you are writing.

(*Guidance note: as the child is painting, discuss how they are feeling*)

So you have finished. Good job – well done. Now think about how you would like to repaint this room. You might like to have another look in the small room to get some ideas about colours. You can choose just one colour or you might like to use more. When you are ready choose the paint and start painting the walls – covering up all those untrue words, phrases and sentences.

As you paint, you feel a sense of letting go and feel so much better inside of you. You know those things that were said were not true. They made you feel a certain way but all the feelings are going now as you paint over each word. You don't have those feelings anymore – they are no use to you at all. Just get rid of them completely – paint them away – and be left with a fresh, clean room.

Now this is a fresh start for you. Make this room somewhere you would like to come back to – where you can relax and feel calm. So the next thing you need to do is look at the four walls and the ceiling – do you need to put in any windows so you can look out to a lovely view?

Now what would you like to have in this room? Some furniture perhaps – what will you bring in?

What else do you need to bring in to make this room comfortable and safe for you? (*Possible prompts: pictures; photos; possessions; people; animals; toys*)

What a lovely room this is now.

From now on you are going to think positive thoughts whenever you come into this room. You know you have the ability not to let words hurt you anymore. You know you are (*insert words appropriate for the child to embed e.g. strong; thoughtful; caring; funny; determined; positive*).

(*Guidance note: the hypnotherapist can also introduce some positive statements/ mantras e.g. I believe in myself; I can speak out; I can challenge: I am who I am*)

Chapter 30

The bakery

Introduction

This script should not be used with a child who is a fussy eater or who has an eating disorder. It works really well with a child who likes their food and drink, or perhaps enjoys cooking and baking.

The main objective is to help the child resolve an issue by considering what would help them to change things and achieve their goal. The script can be used in a creative way so that the child feels in control and creates their own solution to a problem. Although the script is solution-focussed, it can be used solely to focus on the child's wellbeing by encouraging them to find the special ingredients they need to improve how they live life now and what they want for the future.

My preference is for a child to decide what they want to bake (rather than the hypnotherapist being prescriptive by suggesting making a pizza or a cake) and for them to add the necessary ingredients. The idea is that the child will add proper food like ingredients but then add special ingredients that are going to help with the issue they are working on. As the food is cooking, the special ingredients will expand. So to illustrate how this might be undertaken, I have also included a simple script about a banana cake.

The script

There is a really good bakery that is not like other bakeries in that it does not have a shop window. It is not on a main street either; you have to walk down a cobbled alleyway to get to it. Once you go down the alleyway you find yourself in a large yard which contains all sorts of different buildings. The bakery is on the left-hand side. It has a big metal door.

The bakery caters for everyone. You can pop in for a quick drink; you can have breakfast, brunch, lunch or tea. Many people who work locally prefer to buy things to take out. I would like you to imagine some of the lovely things that you can buy.

All different types of breads: loaves of all shapes and sizes; long, short, round and square.

Cakes: big cakes for special occasions or little cakes for a special treat.

Sandwiches and wraps: choose whatever filling you like.

All types of different salads: look at all the gorgeous colours in each salad bowl.

All these beautiful tasty things are made in the kitchen at the bakery. The kitchen is huge and has all sorts of catering equipment, which is stored in cupboards, drawers and some things are hanging on the walls and from the ceiling. There are big cookers, ovens, freezers, fridges and sinks. This kitchen is short of nothing at all; you can *always* find what you need if you look hard enough.

There are lots of cupboards on all the walls going high up to the ceiling, where there is a big window bringing in lots of daylight. You may be able to see the sky and clouds through it if you look up there.

Back in the kitchen you will see spoons, forks, knives, plates, bowls, baking trays, ordinary trays and saucepans.

Now we all know that it is good to eat healthily and have a good diet but sometimes when people are poorly they can only manage to eat certain things – for example, tomato soup when you have a cold; a slice of toast when you have not eaten for a while. Eating these things makes you feel stronger and you get better sooner if you eat or drink something.

Certain foods that you enjoy can make you feel happy – like chocolate cake or a banana milkshake (*or insert something you know the child likes*).

Now what I haven't told you yet is that this is a very special kitchen. Lovely tasty things are made here for the people living and working in the local area but the owner of the bakery lets people come in when the bakery is closed so they can make their own special recipe to make them feel better in any way they want. The owner is a great believer in using your special mind; he thinks that your special mind knows exactly what you need to do and that includes making something with your own special ingredients.

The owner also lets animals come into the bakery when they cannot find the food they need. Harry the Heron, who loves to eat fish, will often come in to make a fish pie to keep his strength up. This is because he sometimes gets very tired when he has to do a lot of flying up and down and round and round. His wings are so huge it takes a lot of effort sometimes to keep flying. So when he is making a fish pie, Harry often puts in one or more special ingredients. When he is tired after a hard day's flying, he puts 'strength' and 'energy' and 'determination to keep going' in his fish pie.

Harry likes to come into the lovely warm kitchen and takes his time making the fish pie. He finds it peaceful in the bakery away from the busy life on the river. Although Harry loves fish he also really likes mashed potato, which is a bit strange for a heron but each to their own taste.

(*Guidance note: at this point the hypnotherapist will work with the child to create anything they want. What follows is a series of prompts that might be used*)

Now you and I have talked about (*insert issue*). I think spending some time cooking in the kitchen of the bakery might be able to help you with (*insert issue*).
What would you like to cook/bake in this kitchen?
What equipment will you need?
Go and have a walk around the kitchen and find the things you need. Look in the cupboards, drawers and on the walls.
What ingredients do you think you might need?
Go and find those ingredients now and get them ready.
What extra special ingredients might you like to put in there?

(Guidance note: at this point the hypnotherapist will suggest ingredients that are relevant to the issue being worked on. Some examples are:

- Courage
- Confidence
- Self-belief
- Self-control
- Good behaviour (or a specific behaviour)
- Calmness
- Stillness
- Peace
- Quiet
- Motivation
- Energy
- Determination
- Concentration
- Positivity
- Happiness
- Excitement.

At this point the hypnotherapist will work with the child to do the cooking/baking. The following additional script illustrates how this can be undertaken)

Additional script 1: Baking a banana cake

OK – so you are going to make a banana cake and you have everything you need to do that right in front of you. Before you start making the cake mixture, don't forget to switch the oven on so it starts to heat up and then it will be ready to bake the cake. Preparation and forward thinking are the key to good baking.

Take the mixing bowl and start putting in some of the ingredients you need – the flour, butter and milk might be a good way to begin. That's right. Then crack some eggs and add them to the mixture. Give them a good stir with a spoon – getting everything blending together – becoming nice and smooth so there are no lumps. Add the sugar next. Keep stirring – good. Now chop up and then mash the bananas and pop them in. Getting the mixture nice and smooth – just as you would like it to be. There are a few other things that are needed to make the cake just right – don't forget the baking powder and baking soda, a little pinch of salt and a small spoonful of cinnamon. Great – you have put all the basic ingredients into the cake mixture, now you need to put in the *very special ingredients* to help you with (*insert issue*).

Have you any ideas about what you might like to put in the cake?

(Guidance note: at this point the hypnotherapist will encourage the child to think about what they need to resolve the issue; if necessary the hypnotherapist can also suggest ingredients that are relevant to the issue being worked on. Some examples are:

- *Courage*
- *Confidence*

- *Self-belief*
- *Self-control*
- *Good behaviour (or a specific behaviour)*
- *Calmness*
- *Stillness*
- *Peace*
- *Quiet*
- *Motivation*
- *Energy*
- *Determination*
- *Concentration*
- *Positivity*
- *Happiness*
- *Excitement)*

So the cake mixture is ready; it has all the *very special ingredients* in it. So spoon the mixture from the bowl into the cake tin and then pop it into the oven. Switch the timer on.

You have worked hard making the cake mixture, so why don't you sit down for a while and perhaps have a drink. Now as the cake is baking, just think of the *very special ingredients* you have put in (*repeat the ingredients*). As the oven is baking those ingredients, imagine them expanding and making the cake rise (*repeat each ingredient again*). The oven is baking the cake so all the ingredients work well together to make it taste just right.

Listen out for the timer; it will ring when the cake is ready. Tell me when you hear it. OK – so take the cake out of the oven and then very carefully turn it out onto a wire cooling tray. Are your taste buds working well – are they eager to taste the cake?

The cake is ready. Now think about those *very special ingredients* you have put in as you cut a slice of the cake (*repeat each ingredient again*). Taste the cake now – and as you chew it and then swallow you feel (*repeat each ingredient again*) growing inside you. So eat as much as the cake as you like but make sure you leave a little slice of it.

When you have finished eating this delicious banana cake, find some foil and a cake tin. Wrap up the remaining slice and put it in the cake tin to keep it really fresh. Find a place in the kitchen to put the cake tin. You can come back to the kitchen in the bakery to taste the cake or make something else if you would like to do so.

There is just one other thing you need to know about this cake. It has a special ingredient in it that makes sure that there is always enough cake and it is never finished. So the cake will always be there for you to eat. All you have to do is say 'banana' to yourself and you will feel (*mention the ingredients again*) baking inside you.

Chapter 31

The climbing wall

Introduction

The main objective in using this script is to help a child achieve a goal or several goals as appropriate. It is important that the climbing wall is seen as a fun activity *not* as a test or hard work in any way.

The script can help a child make a decision about what they want to do, whether it be in relation to a specific problem or dilemma (e.g. in relation to the best way forward; which direction to take regarding choice of school, subjects to take), or more simply what would make them happy and improve their wellbeing. The script works well especially if the child has been unsure about something or they have been lacking confidence in their ability to do something. The idea is to help the child set realistic goals and have time to think about how they are going to achieve what they want or need to do.

The script encourages the child to revisit the climbing wall to help them achieve their goals over time. It is important to stress that there is no expectation that everything has been done at once. After using the script the first time, and if the hypnotherapist is seeing the child for more sessions, I think it is really useful to use the script again to review progress.

Before using the script, the hypnotherapist should check out that a child does not have a fear of heights and it would not work well with a child who does not enjoy sports or physical activity.

The script

Now all of us at some time or other find something difficult to do or we struggle to get something finished, but if you really want to do something you will do it with motivation and determination. It can be helpful to set yourself targets or small goals and see how you progress. Nothing has to be done in a rush – small steps are good.

There is a place that has a climbing wall. This is where people who like climbing outdoors come for fun when they do not have time to go further afield – like into the countryside. When people are climbing the wall, they are having fun and it can give them time to think about all sorts of things.

The climbing wall can help you achieve. It can help you make decisions, set goals and gives you time to think about how you are going to go about achieving whatever it is you want to do.

So I want you to imagine the climbing wall. It is very high but also very wide. It has funny shaped things sticking out; people who climb the wall can hold these things and put their feet on them. They are called climbing holds. There are different pathways up the wall – some people call them routes. Can you see (*or sense*) them?

Before you start your climb, I would like you to find a table where you can sit down and look at the wall. You will see that there is a large sheet of paper with a sticky back, pens and scissors on the table. Keep looking at the wall and think about what you want to achieve (*insert an issue if already discussed*).

Think about your goals – what you want to achieve. Be very specific if you can. Just take your time to think – there is no rush at all. When you are ready tell me about your goals.

(Guidance note: the hypnotherapist should ensure that the child does not set too many goals. The goals should be realistic. It is important that the child does not set him/herself up to fail)

Take the paper which is on the table and start cutting it up into smaller pieces. For each goal you have chosen write it down on one of the pieces of paper and then fold it up. When you have written something on a piece of paper please tell me what it is – I would be very interested to hear.

(Guidance note: discuss each goal in turn with the child and make sure they are realistic. The hypnotherapist may make some suggestions to help the child)

Now you need to get ready for your climb. You will need a harness and some rope. Can you find them? Put them on. Another really useful bit of equipment to have is a chalk bag. The chalk keeps your fingers and palms of your hands dry if you get a bit hot and sweaty at any time. Find your chalk bag and tie it around your waist. Now get your pieces of folded paper and decide where you are going keep them (*prompt if necessary e.g. in a pocket; under a belt; in the chalk bag*), so that you can pull them out as you climb the wall.

Look up at the wall and decide which way you are going to go – which route are you going to take? Look at the way you are going to go and you might like to think about where you are going to place your bits of paper with your goals on the route you take. I wonder if you want to put them in any particular order – it is really up to you.

You are now beginning to feel excited about starting your climb. You know the direction you are going to take. You are very determined that you are going to get to the top of the wall. It does not matter how long you take to reach the top – you will get there. Feel that determination. Think how good you are going to feel when you have successfully reached the top. What an achievement it will be.

Are you ready to start your climb? Right – start your climb now and just stop when you want to place one of your goals on the wall. Tell me when you stop to place one of your goals.

(Guidance note: encourage the child to tell you when they stop and what goal they are placing where)

Take pleasure from climbing up the wall but also enjoy the feeling of being higher up and proud of what you are achieving – climbing to the very top. How good you are feeling. What an achievement going higher and higher. You are doing so well. You realise that you can do anything if you really are determined. You are nearly there now. When you get to the top – sit on top of the wall – and take a rest. Feel proud of yourself for getting to the very top.

Just rest for a while. Feel good about yourself and what you have achieved. Now think about each of the goals you have stuck on the wall. They won't come off the wall – the sticky paper will keep them there – safe and secure.

When you are ready you need to climb back down the wall. Again there is no need to rush. Do things in your own time. Take it steady and easily and tell me when you are back on the ground.

Well done. You climbed up the wall, placed your goals where they needed to be and you successfully climbed back down the wall. What an achievement. Take a step back and look at the wall. Look at where you have placed your goals. For each goal think about these questions:

What do I need to do to achieve this/make this happen?
What do I need to plan for?
What do I need to organise?

(Guidance note: the hypnotherapist needs to leave plenty of time for this activity)
Are you ready to climb the wall again? Start climbing when you are ready. Stop at each goal and tell me your plans – how you will achieve that goal.
(Guidance note: talk through each goal repeating the questions above as prompts if necessary)
Well done again – that was a great climb. You deserve another rest on the top of the wall. While you are sitting there so comfortably, I want you to know that it is not necessary to do everything at once. You can take your time and do things at your own pace – no need to rush. Just like climbing the wall – you can do it very quickly or very slowly. It really doesn't matter. You have to do what is right for you. Focusing on one goal at a time; maybe focussing on two goals – it is really up to you. You don't have to do everything at once.

You can come back to the climbing wall any time you like to climb the wall again, look at your goals and see how you are doing. You can always change the way you climb the wall just like you can change the way you are going to achieve your goals. Each time you climb the wall you will feel that great sense of achievement. Returning regularly to the climbing wall will increase your determination to achieve your goals. When you come back to the wall, look at your goals and see how you are progressing. Feel that great sense of achievement.

Chapter 32

Bennett's Bicycle Shop

Introduction

I wrote this script specifically for children who struggle with learning and doing any form of test or exam. They want to do well, put in the hard work but they do not believe in themselves. They set themselves up to fail because they do not believe they can succeed or they convince themselves they are going to forget what they have learnt or will not be able to recall the information they need.

The script can be used with really young children in infant/junior schools (who have to face all sorts of tests even at such a young age), but also those younger people who are facing their GSCEs or A levels. I find that even though some young people have had really good results at GSCE level, they still lack confidence or have a fear that their memory is going to let them down.

Although the script is aimed to focus on remembering for academic purposes, it can be used for other situations a child might become nervous about. Outside of school the child may be taking other types of exams e.g. piano, dance or for an older teenager a driving test. There could be other situations in which the child has to perform and thinks they will forget what is expected of them e.g. forgetting the words when taking part in a play or singing in a choir or performing solo; forgetting the steps or routine when dancing in a show.

Therefore the main objectives of the script are to build a child's confidence; for them to believe in themselves but also to acknowledge that the hard work they have put in learning something (whether it be knowledge or a particular skill) is stored in the subconscious and can be retrieved when needed.

I have also added a small additional script after the main script which can be used as an introduction to trance and to demonstrate the power of the imagination in a first session, because I know so many children enjoy taking a bicycle ride.

The script

There are lots of different ways to travel and you know that your imagination can take you anywhere you want to go. Today I want you to think about bicycles, because I want to tell you about a very interesting bicycle shop.

Imagine that you are standing outside The Bicycle Shop; in the window you can see all sorts of bicycles – big and small – for girls and boys of all different ages. Do you see one you like? There are plenty more inside to choose from, so why don't you go through the door? Now have a look around.

The man who owns this shop is called Mr Bennett. He is a very clever man because as well as selling bicycles he can also mend them. Lots of children come to his shop with all sorts of different problems – when a chain has broken; a tyre has got a puncture; the brakes are not working as well as they should. Sometimes all the children really want to do is talk to Mr Bennett, because he always listens and gives good advice. I'd like to tell you about how he helped a little boy called Arlo.

Arlo came to the shop one day and said there was a problem with the brakes on his bicycle. After giving the bicycle a good going over Mr Bennett knew straight away the brakes were working perfectly. He asked Arlo to sit down while he continued to tinker around with the bicycle. He knew given some time that Arlo would tell him the real reason he had come into the shop.

Arlo started to talk about how he found writing at school very hard and he dreaded every Monday morning when his teacher gave the class a spelling test. Arlo said he did always do his homework and did his best to learn the words but he was always scared he would forget how to spell them correctly. This resulted in him feeling sick every Sunday night when he went to bed and he did not want to get up to go to school the next day. He could never eat breakfast on a Monday morning. Of course he had to go to school but on the way there he would start to feel even worse. He would get horrible feelings in his tummy, which made him feel even sicker than the night before, and his legs would get so wobbly he felt like he was going to fall over.

Mr Bennett said that everyone – both children and adults – gets nervous about something. Mr Bennett said when he had been at school he had struggled learning his times tables and he himself had always found pumping up tyres was helpful. 'Pumping up tyres – how does that help?' asked Arlo. Mr Bennett suggested he sit back and closes his eyes and he would explain:

> Now just imagine that your bicycle's tyres need some air putting in them. Just look at those two tyres – they are looking a bit flat. Now imagine it is Sunday night and you are thinking about the spelling test tomorrow. Focus on how you are feeling – all those horrible feelings you told me about inside your tummy.
>
> Now look again at the front tyre on your bicycle – it is looking a bit flat, but let's see if you can make it even flatter. Look for the valve on the tyre – when you have found it take off the little cap. Now wiggle the valve about and let the air out. As the air comes rushing out imagine it is blowing away all those horrible feelings in your tummy and feel them rushing out of the tyre. As the tyre gets flatter and flatter, all those horrible feelings are leaving your tummy. That is such a good feeling.
>
> Now let out the air in the back tyre – watch it getting flatter and flatter and any horrible feelings you have left in your tummy are leaving. By the time the back tyre is completely flat your tummy is completely empty of those horrible feelings.
>
> Now get the pump ready to fill the tyres with fresh, new air. Imagine pumping air into the front tyre and as you see the tyre filling up imagine you are in the classroom feeling confident about the spelling test. Feel that confidence building

up inside of you. You know you have done the work and your special mind will remember those spellings. Pump away, watch the tyres get bigger and bigger; they become firm and reliable. As you are pumping the air into the tyre you are feeling more and more confident. Fantastic.

You might like to feel the tyre to see if it is firm enough. If it does need any more air just put some more in until it feels just right – firm and reliable.

When you have finished pumping up the front tyre, go to the back tyre and start pumping air into that. Feel that confidence growing again and as you continue to fill the tyre with air, feel the confidence growing and imagine what it feels like when you get your spellings right. How good does that feel? Be proud of yourself. Well done.

When you are ready check that back tyre and make sure it is firm and reliable.

Good. Both tyres are ready to take you on a ride wherever you want to go. You have prepared the tyres for a journey. They are firm and reliable. Those tyres are like you in a way. You put in the work and learn those words – preparing for your spelling tests. Just like the tyres are ready to go on a journey you are ready to do those spelling tests. Your memory – like the tyres – will not let you down. You are on the road to success.

Additional script 1: Going for a ride

Now a bicycle can take you anywhere you want to go in your imagination. So just check your bicycle – make sure it is safe and ready to ride. Check the tyres, brakes, pedals and chain are all in good working order. That's right. Now give the saddle a polish. Get yourself seated in a comfortable position on that saddle and be ready to push off. Take a nice big, deep breath and push off.

Start pedalling – round and round the pedals go – going forward smoothly. I wonder if you might like to go a little faster. Or maybe you want to go slower. It is really up to you. Make the bicycle go at the speed that is just right for you. That's good.

Now this is a very special bicycle – it has magical powers. Like ordinary bicycles it can go forwards or backwards; it can turn right or left. But this magical bicycle can also go up and down, turn somersaults – it can do anything you want it to do. So would you like to try that out? Make the magical bicycle rise up off the ground. Take it as high as you like. Going higher and higher. Now make it go down – and down and down. I wonder what else you can make it do. What about spinning? – round and round and round. Rocking – forward, backwards and sideways. Jumping – how high can it go? What is it jumping over?

Have fun with the bicycle. Let the bicycle take you anywhere you want to go or let it take you on a magical mystery tour.

Chapter 33

Storing and recalling

Introduction

I meet so many children who say they cannot remember things or they tell me they have a bad memory. That belief is reinforced by the negative word 'can't' being repeatedly used and the lack of belief in self. Therefore, it is important that a child (of any age) learns that everything is stored in their subconscious mind and there is a way of finding information. So the two scripts below are to help a child who has a problem with:

- Remembering things
- Studying
- Revising
- Exam anxiety.

Please note when using Script 1 that a child may not see their reliable librarian as a person but rather an animal or an object. The most recent example from my own practice at the time of writing is the reliable librarian presented as a huge paperclip.

The purpose of Script 2 is to demonstrate that it is possible to recall things from a long time ago if the child relaxes and does not panic about not being able to remember. The emphasis is on letting things happen naturally. It proves to the child that they can remember things from a long time ago. The hypnotherapist can then move on to work with a difficulty that the child is regularly experiencing (e.g. remembering spellings, times tables, dates in history or names of rivers) or a memory they want to recall or an incident that needs to be relived for therapeutic purposes. I use this script when working with children who have experienced abuse and we are working through the healing process.

I have included an additional script for the hypnotherapist who specifically wants to use regression techniques. This script can be used after using script 1 or 2, or it can be used as a stand-alone. There are so many different ways to regress a child, but this script will appeal to the child who likes books and enjoys reading.

Script 1: The library

When I say the word 'library' I wonder what you think of first. Some people think of books straight away but others might think of a library of music – old vinyl records, cassette tapes, CDs. A library could be a collection anything – recipes, maps, stamps, spoons, dolls, toy cars, teddy bears – anything at all.

A library can store masses of information in lots of different ways. Your special mind stores lots of things. It remembers everything you have ever heard, seen, said, read, learnt or done. So sometimes you may think you have forgotten something but you have no need to worry because it is stored safely somewhere in your special mind. You just need to find the best way to get to it. So that is why I would you like you to think about your very own unique library – the library in your special mind.

So just imagine that you are walking along a main road in a town or city. I bet you can see shops – cafes – maybe a hotel. It is an ordinary kind of day so there are probably lots of people about – adults – children – maybe some animals – some traffic. What do you see?

Keep on walking – you just know the right way to go in order to find your library. Take your time, there is no rush – just tell me when you see a building that you know is your library.

Tell me what your library looks like. Is it old or modern? What is it made of? How many floors does it have? Are there any windows? Is there just one entrance or are there more? Go up to the main entrance and stand in front of the door. What is it made of? What colour is it? Look above the top of the door – you will see a huge sign saying (*insert child's name*) Library.

When you are ready open the door and go into your library. As you are going in there remember that libraries can store masses of information in different ways. Children and adults learn in all sorts of ways and they can remember things in unusual ways too – ways that suit them best. Everyone needs to find ways and things to help them *learn* and *remember*. Some people like books and reading; others learn better by watching something – like on a DVD or a programme on the television or a video on YouTube. The internet has lots of information too. Others like to watch a demonstration or some prefer to talk to a person in order to learn how to do something.

Every person in this world is good at something and everyone can get better at doing things if they really want to do so. So it is important to find out the best way you *learn* and *remember* things. This is how the library in your special mind can help.

So now you need to find things in your library which will help you *learn* and *remember* in the future.

Imagine you are standing in the reception area of the library. You will be able to see how many floors there are up to the very top and you will also see if there is a way down to the basement. There will be a staircase and also a lift somewhere so you can go to the rooms you need whenever you want. There are lots of rooms in your library because it stores all the things you have learnt since the moment you were born right up to what you have been learning very recently. So there are a lot of things stored in here.

Your special mind has stored information in a very special way and you can access that information anytime you want to do so. The rooms also contain aids and equipment to help you: books; articles; notes you have written; pens; paper; post-it notes; postcards; computers; iPads; television screens; headphones (*add in anything else you know the child uses*).

In addition, there are rooms with things to help you feel good – like a kitchen with your favourite foods and drinks; a relaxation room where you can take some time out from studying and (*suggest something that you know is related to an interest the child has e.g. a gym to work out and get fit; a music room to listen or play music/instruments*). There may be other rooms that you know you need and you can make them just as you want them to be.

Before exploring these rooms you need to find your very own reliable librarian to show you where everything is. So walk further into the library to the reception desk – you will find your reliable librarian there. Who or what do you find? Say 'hello' to your reliable librarian and introduce yourself. Ask (*him/her/it*) if they have a name. Explain how pleased you are that they are there to help you find your way around. Now with your reliable librarian to guide you, the two of you are going to take a look at some of the rooms.

Remember your library is storing everything you have ever heard, seen, said, read, learnt or done. It is all here for you to remember at any time. Things you have learnt at home, nursery and school. You have learnt in other places too – when out and about with family or friends – on school trips – and holidays. You never ever stop learning and the library in your special mind stores everything you have ever heard, seen, said, read, learnt or done. It is all there, safely stored for whenever you need it.

Now go and explore your library. Look into the rooms and tell me what you see. How are things stored?

(Guidance note: it is important at this point to let the child explore and for the hypnotherapist to follow their lead. It can be useful to use some prompts/ask questions if necessary – some examples given below)

- Books
- Articles
- Notes
- Essays
- Projects
- DVDs
- Films
- Pictures/drawings/diagrams
- Documentaries
- A previous teacher
- Someone they admire
- A classroom the child liked.

So now you have become familiar with where everything is stored. Just have a think about whether you need to change or reorganise anything. You will know the best and easiest way for you to remember things. Do you like to have things in date order or maybe you like things to be in subject order or do you have a special way of organising things? You choose what is best for you, and reorganise anything now if you need to do so. Maybe think about the information you might need in the very near future and make it easy to get to. Do you need to put some of it in a room which is nearer or on a different floor? Think about where is best for you to store things. Then you will remember where everything is stored and you will be able to get to it easily and quickly.

So when you have sorted everything out and the information in your library is stored just as you want it to be – easily and quickly accessible – thank your reliable librarian for helping you. The reliable librarian will always be there to help you find information – you just have to ask (*him/her/it*), and you can come back to the library anytime you need to get some stored information. It does not matter where you are. You can always access the library in your special mind.

Anything you learn in the future will automatically be stored securely and will be easily accessible. When you study or revise for exams you may develop a new way of learning or remembering. Your library will store these new ways and techniques. Rest assured everything is stored safely and is easily and quickly accessible.

So feel confident knowing that everything is stored safely, and is easily and quickly accessible in the library in your special mind. You do not have to worry about anything at all.

Script 2: The archives

I don't know if you have ever heard of 'archives' or know what they are, but I would like to explain about them because your special mind has archives – and you could use them to help you remember things.

You already know that your special mind is very clever and that you have a fantastic imagination – it can take you wherever you want to go. Your special mind does lots of other things too and one of the most important jobs it does is to help you remember things. So let's go back to the word 'archives'. Simply, an archive is a place where you can store things – maybe something important that needs to be kept safe for a very long time. Archives can store old things – like memories.

Now your special mind knows everything about you – yes it does. Your special mind remembers everything you have ever heard, seen, said, read, learnt or done. It keeps everything safe. So when you want to remember something you can – if you just relax and think about what you need to remember. There is no need to force things, just let things come naturally.

Your special mind will store things in a way that is best for you. It will divide things up and put them in different places for safe keeping. Think of all the stories you can remember or the lines of nursery rhymes you can recite or songs you can sing – without really thinking or trying. Have you ever wondered how you can remember so much? Well it is all down to your special mind. Your special mind archives what you have learnt and what you might need to remember in the future.

So it might be exciting to take a tour of the archives in your special mind.

Now just let your mind drift. Think about the different places where things could be stored: a room perhaps; a cellar; a loft; a drawer; a cupboard; a wardrobe; a suitcase; a box; a shelf; a desk; a filing cabinet. Can you think of anywhere else?

What do the archives in your mind look like? Where does your special mind store things?

The archives in your special mind have lots of room and storage space.

Let's see how good your special mind can be at remembering things. It is a long time since you were a baby, isn't it? Maybe you don't remember much about being a baby, but you had lots to learn back then. You had to learn to do lots of things which you take for granted now – drinking, eating, going to the toilet, crawling, walking and talking. All these things come so naturally now you don't have to give them any thought at all.

So find the baby room in the archives and see what is in there. See the things that helped you learn to drink, eat, go to the toilet, crawl, walk and talk.
(Guidance note: when the child says what they see the hypnotherapist should encourage them to talk about what they remember doing/learning; keep emphasising how easy it is to remember. The following prompts can be used)

Baby

- Plastic bottle, spoon, cup
- Potty
- Reins
- Car seat
- Safety locks
- Safety gates.

School

- Books
- Pencils, pens, crayons, paints
- Playdough, Plasticine
- Lego
- Pictures
- Numbers.

(Guidance note: at this point the hypnotherapist can:

- *Go to other times in the child's life to illustrate that they can remember things* OR
- *Use regression to recall something the child says they need to remember* OR
- *Regress to a specific incident and release the feelings associated with it)*

So start looking around your archives and find the room that stores *(insert memory/ specific incident)*.

Additional Script 1: Books and messages

Start looking around your library/archives and find the room that only has books in it. Tell me when you have found it.

Now go into the room and you will see shelves on all the walls. All the shelves go from the floor right up to the ceiling. Holding so many books of all shapes, sizes and colours. Some are hardbacks and some are paperbacks. I know you like books so go and have a look along the shelves. Take your time wandering around the shelves *(let the child take his/her time – then prompt)*.

Can you see any specific titles?
What are they?
Are you drawn to a particular book?

Would you like to have a closer look?
Look at the book you have chosen.

(Guidance note: the hypnotherapist can then choose how to proceed)

Tell me what it looks like. On the count of 3 I want you to open the book and see if there is a message inside for you – 1, 2, and 3.

(Guidance note: the hypnotherapist can then work with this message if there is one)

OR

This book is an autobiography. It is a book about your life. Now this book is a bit different to other books. You start reading it from the back – not the front. So just turn to the back page and start reading it. It tells you all about what you have done today since waking up this morning.

Why don't you find something to sit on in this special room of books? Make yourself comfortable so you can have a good read. Take the book with you. Just relax as you start reading backwards through the pages. As you are reading you become more and more relaxed. So keep on reading going back through: today; yesterday; last week; last month; the last three months; the last six months; the last year.

(Guidance note: the hypnotherapist has two options how to proceed from this point onwards:

- *Count through the child's age/years and stop at an age when a known event needs to be worked on*

OR

- *Let the child drift back and let them decide where to stop in the book)*

Tell me what you are reading about in the book about you.

What you are doing?
What do you look like?
Where are you exactly?
Is anyone with you?
How are you feeling?
What happens next?

Chapter 34

The spa

Introduction

The spa is another script I developed when working with a particular exam anxiety group. All the group members were experiencing panic attacks, which manifested in getting over-heated and then sweating profusely. So that is how the script started – using the sauna, steam room and mountain of crushed ice to reduce body temperature. Over the years the script has been developed further to deal with issues members of other exam anxiety groups have presented.

What is offered below is the spa with the 'facilities' that I use most with members of exam anxiety groups. The hypnotherapist may not want to use all of the facilities and of course s/he can always add further facilities which might be of interest and helpful to the child.

I have found that it is also appropriate to use the script with individual children. The script aims to deal with anxiety and physical problems related to it. The main objective in using the swimming pool is to help the child leave things behind – whether it is a specific problem, thought, feeling or memory. The lounge is a place to relax but the television can be used for forward pacing to work on a particular issue and embed commands/suggestions by using the television screen in the lounge.

The script

Just imagine that you are standing in a large car park. Look around you. See the lorries, coaches, cars, vans, maybe some motorbikes. As you are looking around you realise that there is a hotel very nearby. Can you see it? Tell me what it looks like. What else can you see around you?

Now this hotel has a spa attached to it and it has a separate entrance to the main reception area. Take a walk towards the hotel now and see if you can find the entrance to the spa. Look out for a sign that says 'The Spa'. Take your time but tell me when you have got there. Are you standing outside the door? What does the door look like? Is anything written on the door or the wall? Now on the count of three I want you to open the door and go into the spa – 1, 2, and 3.

Take a nice deep breath and look around you. Somewhere you will see a reception desk and there will be a person there – a receptionist – to help you. Feel in your pocket and you will find a special voucher which you need to give to the receptionist. On the voucher it says: 'Special Guest: Can Visit Anytime'. When you are ready walk towards the reception desk. Greet the receptionist and show him/her the voucher. Does the receptionist tell you his/her name or are they wearing a name badge perhaps? The receptionist (*use name if one has been given*) will now show you around the spa, so you know what facilities are available.

Just keep breathing nice and slowly as you explore – walking slowly down a corridor – looking through the doors and windows.

First of all you are shown the changing rooms. There may be lots of things there for you: lockers for your clothes and belongings; towels; robes and slippers; showers; toilets; washbasins; hairdryers; hand-dryers; shower gel; shampoo; hair conditioner; moisturiser and hand cream. What can you see? Can you smell anything?

The receptionist leaves you for a while so you can get changed into something you feel comfortable with and s/he also gives you a robe to wear. So just get yourself ready and say when you are ready for the receptionist to show you the rest of the spa.

Walk down the corridor and at the far end you see a gym. Through the glass window you can see people are working hard on all the different equipment. Some are running on treadmills; others are pedalling fast on bicycles and others are lifting weights.

To the left is another corridor and you see a sign to the swimming pool. You go through a door marked 'Swimming Pool' and in front of you there is a very long swimming pool. Some people are swimming very slowly and gently; others are swimming really fast. What can you hear? What can you smell? You can come back for a swim later if you would like to do so.

Come out of the swimming pool area and walk down another corridor. You walk into another place. On one side there are two doors. The receptionist opens the first door and you feel the dry heat hit you. This is the sauna. Have a look in. Go in – sit or lie on one of the wooden benches. Feel the dry heat going into the pores of your skin relaxing you. How hot is it? Is anybody else in there with you? When you have had enough come out and go to the next door.

Here is the steam room. Again the receptionist opens the door to show you but you cannot see much as the room is full of steam. You feel hot again but it is different this time – it is a damp heat. Would you like to go in? Go in – sit or lie down on the tiled seats. Feel the wetness go into the pores of your skin relaxing you.

Feel yourself getting hotter and hotter and hotter. The heat seems to be increasing even more so – it is becoming unbearably hot. Hotter and hotter. It is so hot now you have to come out of the steam room.

As you rush out, the receptionist closes the door to the steam room. You turn around and you see a huge mountain of crushed ice. As you walk towards the mountain of crushed ice you see the bottom of it has been built into a sunken bath and then it rises upwards – very high. The ice has magical powers to cool you down very quickly anytime you feel very hot and sweaty (*or insert physical symptoms experienced by the child if known*) when you are feeling anxious (*or insert appropriate emotion experienced by the child*). So just try it out now. Maybe you would like to pick up some of the ice and feel how cold it is but also how refreshing it is. Maybe you would like to rub some of it onto your arms or face – wherever you are feeling hot.

Stretch your arms out in front of you and let your fingertips touch the mountain of crushed ice – see how cool it feels. Then sink your fingers, thumbs into the mountain; go a little deeper and further down into the cold ice. Your hands are now completely in the ice right up to your wrists. If you want to, push your arms right down into the ice – maybe up to your elbows or even your shoulders. How good does that feel? All the time you are feeling cooler and cooler throughout your whole body as your arms go deeper and deeper into the mountain of crushed ice.

As your body cools down you are beginning to feel calmer and calmer. Anytime in the future when you need to cool down you know you can come back to the spa with your special voucher and use the mountain of crushed ice.

(Guidance note: at this point the hypnotherapist can continue with the receptionist showing the child the following facilities or add their own or leave the spa)

The swimming pool

Imagine that you are walking into the swimming pool area. There is no-one else there – just you. It is very peaceful. All you may hear is the gentle movement of the water in the pool. See the swimming pool; make yourself aware of the shallow end and then the deep end. See where there are steps down into the pool. See the diving board – high above the water. There are some chairs around the pool, so if you have a towel with you just find somewhere to put it and maybe you would like to leave your robe and slippers there too.

Walk up to the edge of the pool at the shallow end. Curl your toes around the edge. Look down into the water and see the colour of the tiles which are on the bottom of the pool and on the sides. Maybe you can see some holes that are the drains which filter the water and keep it clean. Dip your toe into the water to see what the temperature is like. Now it is time to go in. How would you like to get into the pool? Jump, dive or go down the steps? Well in you go now.

Now imagine that you are going to do the breaststroke. Nice smooth, relaxing movements – no need to rush. Your arms and legs move you gently through the water. Just get into a nice steady rhythm – pushing gently through the water.

It is so relaxing to have a gentle swim. Just let any thoughts or worries you have leave you. Just swim away from anything that has been troubling you (*insert a relevant issue/thought/feeling/memory to the child*). With each stroke you become more and more relaxed – calmer and calmer. You are leaving (*the issue/emotion*) further and further behind you.

Keep swimming slowly and gently – up and down the length of the pool. Just keep going – that's it. Feeling good, relaxed and calm. Keep on swimming until you have left (*the issue/emotion*) far behind – until you are thinking about nothing at all – leave everything behind you. You are feeling good, relaxed and calm.

The lounge

There is a lounge in the spa which is another place in which you can relax. You can do absolutely nothing or you may choose to use some of things this lounge has to offer you. So just go in now and have a look around.

Look at the different types of chairs and sofas there are; all shapes, sizes and colours. Tell me what you see. Which chair or sofa might suit you best?

Somewhere you will see a table full of refreshments: water, fruit juices, tea and coffee. There are also some biscuits, cakes and fruit.

You will see somewhere some books and magazines. Go and have a look. Is there anything of interest to you?

Somewhere you will find a huge television screen on one of the walls. Can you see it?

Just take what you need to make yourself comfortable and sit yourself down in a chair or on a sofa from where you have a clear view of the television screen. You will find somewhere near to you a remote control for the television. Have you got it?

(Guidance note: the hypnotherapist can then do some forward pacing work to work on a particular issue)

Leaving the spa

Well now it is time to go back to the changing rooms, have a shower and get dressed again. I'll leave you for a while in the changing rooms. Don't forget to use all the facilities and those lovely things that are there for you – shower gel; shampoo; hair conditioner; moisturiser and hand cream. I'll be quiet for a while. You tell me when you are ready to leave.

I hope you have enjoyed your first visit to the spa. Make your way back to the reception desk. Ask the receptionist for your special voucher and put it somewhere safe – so you can use it again in the future. Remember you can come back to the spa anytime you want, whenever you want to relax *(and insert issue to be worked on)*. Thank the receptionist for showing you around. Now make your way back into the car park.

Chapter 35

The igloo

Introduction

This is another script I first developed when running an exam anxiety group. A commonality amongst those particular group members was that they became very hot and sweaty whenever they started thinking about revision, the proximity of the exams or taking the actual exams. Some group members were regularly experiencing severe panic attacks. Since writing the script for that particular group I have used it in other exam anxiety groups when needed.

I also use the script regularly for individual children who are experiencing anxiety and panic attacks which are not related to exams but result in them having problems with their body temperature. They can become very hot or the opposite can also happen i.e. a child can experience shivering and feel very cold when anxious[1]. This script can also help to regulate body temperature when working with general or social anxiety or in specific situations e.g. flying.

The beginning of the script (when the child is imagining walking to the igloo) can be used to relax the child and get him/her to become calmer before teaching how to control their body temperature.

The script

You have told me that when you are (*insert situation*) you get very hot and you experience (*insert how this manifests*). Well I want to help you with that now.

Imagine that you are standing somewhere by yourself, surrounded by beautiful, white, snow that is glistening in the sunshine. Look into the deep snow that is all around you – to the right, to the left, in front of you and behind you. The snow is totally untouched – a perfect white blanket because no-one has walked upon it. It is pure and unspoilt. Being surrounded by this white vision gives you a sense of peace, tranquillity, comfort and safety. The snow is very, very deep indeed. Take a few steps forward and see just how far down your feet go.

Now look up to the bright blue sky and see the sun shining. Take a nice deep breath and enjoy the intake of fresh, clean air as it makes its way down – deep into your lungs. All the time breathing slowly and steadily. Take some more really deep breaths and feel the goodness of the fresh, clean air reaching every part of your body. The fresh clean air feels soothing and calm as it travels all around the inside of your body.

Now start walking forwards – enjoying the sense of peace, tranquillity, comfort and safety as you go. You are becoming calmer and more relaxed with every step that you take – as your feet sink deep down into the snow.

As you go further forward you see something in the distance, but you cannot make out what it is yet. You are curious – so just keep walking forward. Eventually the shape becomes clearer. You realise that the shape in front of you is like a dome – and then you realise it is an igloo – what some people call a snow hut.

Eskimos live in igloos and they are usually very warm inside because the snow being tightly packed keeps the heat in. The temperature in the igloo in front of you can be changed whenever you want; it can help you to feel cooler when you get very hot – like when you are feeling panicky (*or insert other emotion*). Or if you are ever very cold, it can help you to warm up. So let's see how it can help you now.

Before you go into the igloo just check how your body temperature is. How are you feeling right at this moment? Hot, cold or just right? OK – so just imagine that you are feeling really hot – too hot and very uncomfortable. Make your body very hot – perhaps remember the last time you were feeling very hot and uncomfortable (*or insert something the child has told you*).

Now crawl into the tunnel entrance of the igloo; go through the tunnel and into the main part of the igloo. Somewhere on the wall of the igloo you will see a thermostat which controls the temperature of the igloo. Just have a look round and tell me when you have found it. The thermostat is controlled by voice commands. So by using your voice you can be in complete control of the temperature in the igloo, your body temperature and how you feel. All you have to do is tell the thermostat what to do because it will react to your commands which you can say out loud or silently to yourself. Remember you are in complete control.

Just find somewhere to sit or lie down in the igloo. You are still feeling unbearably hot. Maybe some parts of you are feeling clammy and sweaty. Maybe you can feel your heart racing – going far too fast. So now tell the thermostat to make the igloo cold. Feel the temperature dropping. As the igloo is becoming cooler and cooler, so your body temperature drops and you start to feel very comfortable. Feel your breathing slowing down as the temperature drops. Your heart is beating steadily – keeping you calm.

Let's see how cold the igloo can really get. Tell the thermostat to make the igloo freezing cold. The temperature drops rapidly and it is absolutely freezing. Your whole body is shivering. Your eyebrows and hair are turning white.

So now tell the thermostat to make the igloo warmer. Let the temperature rise until it is just perfect for you. Your body temperature feels just right. That's good. You are breathing naturally and your heart is beating steadily – keeping you calm. All is well.

Remember you are always in control. You can change anything you want to change and you now have the igloo and the thermostat to help whenever you feel too hot (*or too cold*). Use your voice to take control. You can just find yourself in the deep, white, glistening snow. Walk towards to the igloo, crawl into the tunnel and tell the thermostat what you want it to do.

Note

1 For a child experiencing shiver or severe cold then the script 'The spa' can be helpful – using the sauna and steam room to warm up.

Chapter 36

Spencer the singer-songwriter

Introduction

Children can lack confidence for any number of reasons. The subconscious remembers everything that have been heard, seen, said and experienced. Negative comments or actions that are repeated frequently by another person can result in a child believing that those comments are true and so embedding negative beliefs about themselves. If a child has witnessed or been subjected to abuse/violence then s/he can find it hard to trust anybody.

For nearly 40 years I have worked with both children and adults who have been abused and have seen the long-term effects of abuse manifest in so many ways. One of the most common effects is the negative image of self: a person believing that they are worthless and/or useless. The story of Spencer the singer-songwriter is a metaphor which can help abused children in particular realise that happiness and success can be found if you do believe in yourself and that it is never too late to heal or succeed.

The script

I want to tell you about Spencer the singer-songwriter because I think you are very like him in some ways. Spencer did not think very much of himself – he had very little confidence and his self-esteem was really low. You'd never think this if you had met him a few years ago. He was very good at putting on a front back then. He always had a lot to say and had an opinion about everything; he sounded confident but he wasn't. He often felt sick inside and sometimes he would have to dash to the toilet to actually be sick.

Spencer was 49 years old and that probably seems very old to you. He had a beautiful singing voice and had always wanted to be a professional singer, but in his mind he did not think he was good enough. Spencer had never thought he was good enough to do anything – even when he was a small boy.

Spencer did not have a very happy childhood. He had seen and heard many horrible things in his house that upset him. After his dad left Spencer and his two brothers, his mum lived with a man who hurt her. Spencer called him 'the intruder'. Spencer saw a lot of things he should never have seen when he was a little boy. It made him very frightened for his mum and for himself and his brothers. He vowed that he would never hurt anyone but also promised himself that he would never ever trust anyone.

He felt that his mum had not protected him or his brothers, and he was really angry with his mum.

Spencer worked hard all his life caring for other people who needed help but in his heart he always wanted to make a career out of singing. He did sing in a band and they did lots of gigs in one particular city but they did not become famous. The problem was they did not promote themselves. Spencer did not believe in himself; he did not think he or the band were good enough. This was all because the intruder frequently told him he was 'useless' when he was a little boy.

Spencer was actually very talented. Not only could he sing beautifully but he could write songs. Songs which had special messages in them. Songs which could help people. He wrote songs about things that were going on in his head. The problem was that Spencer did not believe in himself – he did not think he or his songs were good enough to be performed in public.

One day Spencer met Helen the hypnotherapist and they became good friends. Like lots of people, Helen thought Spencer had a beautiful voice and that singing should be his full-time job. Whenever Helen brought this up, Spencer made excuses: 'I'm too old now' or 'It's too late'. So Helen always said back to him: 'It's never too late', but still Spencer would do nothing about his singing or promoting the songs he had written.

Well if Spencer didn't change his way of thinking, other things did change. Over the next few months some members of the band decided to leave for various reasons and eventually there were no gigs left to do. Spencer was on his own and said again: 'It's too late'. He believed he needed the band members around him; he could not sing on his own.

Helen could not work in her role as a hypnotherapist to help Spencer because they were friends, so she thought about how else she could get Spencer to think differently about himself and build his confidence.

In the city where Spencer lived there is a place called the Orange Gateway where musicians can rent rooms out by the hour to have practice sessions. Musicians get to know each other in this place. Spencer's birthday was coming up so Helen booked some sessions as a present for him – so he could practise singing but also have some peace and quiet to write more songs. She knew that the musicians who used the place were a really friendly bunch who would come to listen to Spencer singing, which is exactly what did happen.

Spencer loved singing the songs he wrote in the room and his beautiful voice was heard by musicians who wanted to play alongside him. They kept telling him how good his voice was and some of the musicians asked if they could play his songs at their gigs.

Spencer had always found it difficult to accept compliments and actually found it very embarrassing. Eventually he did start to trust what the musicians were saying about his voice and his songs. One day a musician told Spencer that some local people were organising an event to raise money for the homeless and they were looking for acts to perform. The musician had put Spencer down to sing one of his songs, which was called 'Believe'.

On the day of the event, Spencer woke up feeling terrible; he was so nervous about singing his song solo in public. He felt like he was going to be sick and he kept going hot and cold. He rang Helen the hypnotherapist and said he just could not sing on his own. Helen came to see Spencer and taught him some breathing exercises. She also kept saying that he should keep saying the first line of his song: '*Believe – Don't let the past hold you back*'.

Spencer still felt nervous as he got up on the stage. His whole body seemed to be shaking and again he kept going hot and cold. So he kept breathing as Helen had taught him to do and repeated to himself: '*Believe – Don't let the past hold you back.*'

After a few more deep breaths Spencer started singing. As he sang he went into a trance. He started to relax and enjoyed singing the song. Gradually, he became aware that people were smiling up at him. Everyone enjoyed listening to his beautiful voice and clapped loudly at the end of the song.

That was the beginning of when Spencer started to believe it was not too late to make changes in his life. He started to sing regularly in public after that and musicians from all over asked if they could sing the songs he had written. A few months later, a man who had seen Spencer perform on stage offered him a recording contract. It was then that Spencer realised that it is never too late to do anything you really want to do and you have to '*Believe – Don't let the past hold you back*'.

Index

abuse 1–3, 11, 13, 16, 18, 20, 35, 75, 82, 98, 103, 118, 130
anchor 7, 15–16, 18, 24, 93
anxiety: disorder 10; general 1, 3, 10–11, 16, 19–20, 69, 124, 128; social 20, 128 *see also* exam
Asperger's syndrome 13, 32
assessment 4–5, 7, 9–10, 12, 17, 21, 27, 30, 46, 90–91
attention deficit hyperactivity disorder (ADHD) 10, 13, 30, 32
autistic spectrum 13, 30, 32

behaviour 5, 13, 17–18, 35, 44, 46, 59, 64–65, 88, 94, 96; cognitive 55; difficult 14; good 110–111; problematic 15, 63; *see also* changing
belief 4, 14, 49, 118; dis- 9; lack of 104; negative 20, 130; self- 14, 18, 49, 103, 110–111, 118
benefits approach 5, 15, 63, 65
bereavement 11, 17, 82–83, 95
breathing 15, 24, 31, 43, 45, 62, 64–65, 67–68, 72, 74, 89, 98, 100–101, 125, 128–129, 132; exercises 16, 24, 71, 73, 131; techniques 20
bullying 1, 11, 16, 18, 71, 75, 103; cyber- 5

Care Act (2014) 3
changing: behaviours 11, 14, 44, 63, 65; feelings 11, 18; thoughts 11
chronic fatigue 10
commands 8–10, 37, 49, 97, 124, 129
confidence 1, 17, 20, 50–51, 58, 75–76, 86, 89, 93, 95, 110, 115–117, 131; boost of 89; lack of 1, 6, 11, 16, 89, 104, 112, 115, 130; self- 4
Continued Professional Development (CPD) 79, 103

death 4, 15, 17, 58, 82–83
deepener 10–11, 13, 17, 39–40, 42, 61
determination 11, 14, 17, 19, 49, 73, 86, 89, 103, 109–114
disability 16, 18, 75

eating disorder 18, 103, 108
education 3–4
Erickson, M. 5
Ericksonian 1, 5
exam anxiety 2, 20, 52, 118; group 2, 14, 20, 24, 44, 124, 128

fear 7, 11, 15–16, 18–20, 53–54, 66–67, 83, 96, 98, 112, 115; freedom from 4
feelings 5, 16–17, 40–41, 44–45, 52, 54, 59, 65–66, 82, 90, 93–94, 96, 100, 107, 122; awareness of 9; bad 68; difficult 14; good 45, 54; horrible 19, 116; of release 18, 97, 101; removal of 13, 18, 20; unwanted 14, 18; *see also* changing
forward pacing 14, 16, 20, 35, 124, 127

Gestalt: methodology 18; therapy 5

habit 5, 11, 16, 18, 69, 96
healing 13, 16, 18, 20, 35, 70, 93, 118
hobbies 4, 7, 21, 91
Hunter, R. 63
Hypnotherapy in Schools Programme (HISP) 2

image 18, 56, 71, 103; negative 11, 130; self- 1, 18, 103
imagination 5, 11–13, 15–16, 19, 21, 27–30, 32–33, 35, 38, 46, 49, 50–51, 58, 62, 67, 70, 73, 79, 115, 117, 121

learning 8, 11, 15, 17, 19–20, 59, 80, 86, 115–116, 119–122
loss 11, 15, 82–83, 95

mantra 14, 16, 20, 49–50, 71; negative 44; training 49
Maslow, A. 4

memories 4, 13, 18, 20, 79, 83–84, 106, 121
mental health 2–4, 89, 91
metaphor 1, 5, 7, 11, 16–17, 19–20, 66, 69, 130
modalities 12, 27
motivation 14, 17, 19, 49, 59, 86, 110–112; lack of 11, 58

panic attack 20, 124, 128
parts therapy 5, 16, 79–80
past life 15, 55–56
phobia 7, 11, 16, 18, 42, 66, 96, 98

rapport 9–10, 12, 21, 30
recalling 11, 19–20
regression 2, 5, 13–14, 16, 18, 20, 35, 38, 55, 66, 118, 122
relationships 4, 21, 91
relaxation 11–13, 15, 24–25, 27, 32, 58, 67, 83, 86, 88, 101, 119

self: -doubt 16; -control 110–111; -esteem 1, 11, 16–17, 20, 75, 103, 130; -portrait 18, 105; -respect 4; -worth 11; -actualisation 4; *see also* belief, confidence, image
sleep 32, 60, 65, 73, 76–77, 84, 94; difficulties 13, 15, 32, 58; disturbed 44; issues 11; -less nights 44; preparation for 32; problems 12, 24; swinging to 15, 58–60; techniques 15
solution focussed approach 5, 55, 66, 108
statements 8–9, 107
storing 19, 120
suggestions 8–10, 18, 32, 51, 113, 124

Tebbetts, C. 63
thoughts 5, 13–14, 20, 25, 45, 59, 87, 93, 96, 126; difficult 14; good 84; intrusive 13, 44; negative 13, 44; positive 107; repetitive 13, 44; unwanted 18; *see also* changing
time: allowing enough 8, 10, 21, 32, 52, 82, 114; forwards in 38; going back in 14–15, 38, 56–57, 67; good 83–84; happy 54; movement of 14; out 5, 32, 61, 94, 119; passing of 52, 54, 76; quiet 13, 33–34; running out 8, 33, 52; slow down 14, 52–54; taking 5, 7, 19, 31–32, 39–41, 43, 52, 56–57, 59–60, 62, 90, 98, 109, 113–114, 119, 124
trance 2, 5, 7–17, 19–21, 24, 30, 32, 35, 4, 46, 56, 58, 61, 63, 72, 76, 82–83, 85–86, 90, 99, 115, 119, 124, 129, 132

wellbeing 1–5, 13, 17, 19, 32, 35, 86–87, 89–93, 103, 108, 112
World Health Organisation 3